Also by Rabbi David Aaron

*Endless Light: The Ancient Path of the
Kabbalah to Love, Spiritual Growth,
and Personal Power*

*Seeing God: Ten Life-Changing Lessons
of the Kabbalah*

THE
Secret Life
of God

DISCOVERING THE
DIVINE WITHIN YOU

Rabbi David Aaron

SHAMBHALA   *Boston & London*   2005

Shambhala Publications, Inc.
Horticultural Hall
300 Massachusetts Avenue
Boston, Massachusetts 02115
www.shambhala.com

Printed in the United States of America

⊗ This edition is printed on acid-free paper that meets the
American National Standards Institute z39.48 Standard.
♻ Shambhala Publications makes every effort to print on recycled paper.
For more information please visit www.shambhala.com.
Distributed in the United States by Random House, Inc.,
and in Canada by Random House of Canada Ltd

The Library of Congress catalogues the previous edition of this book as follows:
Aaron, David, 1957–
The secret life of God: discovering the divine within you/David
Aaron.—1st ed.
p.   cm.
Includes index.
ISBN 978-1-59030-146-3 (hardcover)
ISBN 978-1-59030-239-2 (paperback)
1. God (Judaism)   2. Spiritual life—Judaism.   3. Cabala.   I. Title.
BM610.A248 2004
296.3′11—dc22
2003026571

Special thanks to my true friend Dr. Herb Caskey,
whose generosity made this project possible.
May the study of this book bring great merit to his parents,
Morris and Rose Caskey of blessed memory.

To my parents,
Joe and Luba

To my wife,
Chana

To my children,
Lyadia, Ne'ema, Ananiel, Nuriel,
Yehuda, Tzuriel, and Shmaya

Thank you for your sweet love!

Contents

Acknowledgments

GREAT THANKS to my wife, Chana. Her unconditional love and gentle encouragement have inspired me to rise to challenges, make choices, and grow.

Many, many thanks to my very talented editor, Sarah Rigler, who did an exceptional job in helping me put these secrets into writing. I am also very thankful to Uriela Sagiv for adding her professional touch, giving these ideas even greater clarity.

My deep appreciation to Kendra Crossen Burroughs of Shambhala Publications for her expertise and advice.

I am extremely grateful to the many friends and supporters of the Isralight Institute, whose generosity has provided me with the opportunity to present the ideas of this book. Special thanks to Dr. Herb Caskey, Robby and Helene Rothenberg, Dr. Michael and Jackie Abels, George and Pam Rohr, Steven Alevy, Mitch and Karen Kuflik, Mayer Offman, David and Dena Reiss, Dr. Bob and Sarah Friedman, Moshe and Sarah Hermelin, Aba and Pamela Claman, Robyn Barsky, and Tzvi Fishman for their consistent love and support.

I am also grateful to the many students who have attended my talks, Isralight seminars, and retreats. Your questions, challenges, and receptivity have empowered me to access and share these sacred teachings.

I am forever in debt to my holy teachers, especially Rabbi Shlomo Fischer *shlita,* for all their brilliance and warmth.

Thank you, Hashem. You are the one and only Author. My entire being is filled with joy and gratitude to serve You.

DAVID AARON
Old City, Jerusalem

Introduction

WHEN I WAS A CHILD I had a very intense relationship with God, or so I thought. I can recall many times that I would make deals with Him. I knew He had His hands in everything and could do whatever He wanted. This meant that I needed to get Him on my side.

The funny thing is that I really developed my relationship with God sitting in the bathroom. Please give me a second to explain.

Whenever my parents would go out of the house I would start to worry. For the first couple of hours I would just feel a little tense, but after a while, when I figured they should have been home by now, I would really get nervous. My stomach would then feel sore and I would immediately get the urge to go to the bathroom. It was then and there that I spilled my guts out to God. I would pray that He bring my parents home safely, and I promised that in return I would be the best little kid in the world. Each time I would take upon myself a commitment to do some good deed.

The amazing thing that happened was that my parents would arrive very shortly after that. This seemed to confirm to me that the bathroom was a very special place for meeting God. I believed that for me the bathroom was the sanctuary where God heard my prayers. Others went to synagogue or church, but God and I had a special meeting place in the bathroom.

Sometimes, when within seconds of my prayers my parents would arrive home, I felt that God had manipulated me. I thought to myself (but I knew He read my thoughts), "You knew all along that my parents were about to arrive, and You stalled them. You set me up to get the better deal."

Bargaining seemed to be a big part of my dialogue with God from childhood into adolescence. But finally I couldn't stand living in fear and the constant feeling that to get anything from God there always had to be some kind of self-sacrifice.

Then one day, I finally mustered up the courage to deny God. But even when I stopped believing in God, I nonetheless continued to fear Him.

Often our happiness, confidence, and spiritual growth are stifled by our perception of God. Many people are still living with their childhood God and need to free themselves from His overbearing shadow. The remedy to this problem is to finally, maturely confront the true identity of God and ourselves.

Does the simple reading of the Bible give us the whole picture? Or is there a secret side to God and humanity that will put everything into perspective?

This is what this book is all about. But you are probably wondering who am I to be talking about the secret life of God. How do I know what it is?

For the last twenty-five years I have researched this very issue. I didn't do it to write this book. I did it to heal myself of theophobia—to free my soul from a pervasive fear of God and to find personal enlightenment and happiness. I knew in my heart that I had been dealing with a deity created in my own image, born out of my fears and insecurities. I decided that I needed to find a source that could answer my questions about who is God and why do I exist. I needed a book called *Everything You Always Wanted to Know About God and Yourself, but Were Afraid to Ask.*

In my search I did not find such a book, but I found something better—I found an entire tradition that deals completely with this issue. It is called Kabbalah.

Kabbalah is the mystical interpretation of the Torah, which embodies the teachings of the prophet Moses. It is a tradition consisting of ancient wisdom that reveals the inside story of God and humanity created in the divine image. It exposes the secret life of God and our ultimate purpose on earth. It offers profound answers to deep questions like:

* Why did a perfect God create such an imperfect me?
* If God is so good, why is this world so bad?
* If God is so kind, why is there so much suffering in the world?
* Why do bad things happen to good people?
* Why do I exist at all?
* What does God want from me?
* Can I ever be good enough?
* Does God need me?
* What difference do my choices make?
* Am I free, or is life predetermined?
* If God is all-powerful, then why does He want me to serve Him?
* Why is God referred to as He? Why can't God be female?
* What happened to all the miracles?

To answer some of these questions takes only a chapter, to answer others takes a lifetime.

The answers in this book are not mine. I am just translating the secrets from Kabbalah into a language that anybody can understand. All I want to do is share the incredible relief I experienced when I discovered that God is not who I thought He was. And I want to share the empowerment and awesome joy in getting to know the real me and the real you.

I hope that by the end of this book you will not only have answers, but also have glimpsed the rich treasure trove of wisdom that can lead you straight to the source of all life, love, and happiness.

In the Jewish tradition the essential name of God is called the Tetragrammaton (from the Greek for "four letters")—transliterated from the Hebrew as YHVH (*yod heh vav heh*). As a reminder that God is beyond human grasp, this essential name is never pronounced, even in prayer. The common practice, when speaking colloquially of this name, is to use the Hebrew word *Hashem*, which literally means "the Name." This is what I do in my personal life, and this is the approach I took in my two previous books *Endless Light* and *Seeing God*. But for the purposes of this book—because we are addressing common misunderstandings about God, I felt it would be necessary to use the word *God* to succeed at redefining it and clearing out a lot of the baggage it conjures up for people. Also, to avoid the convolutions of English usage, I reluctantly acceded to using the pronoun *He*, even though (as we will see in chapter 5) it can be very misleading and does not give us the full truth about God.

The subtitle of this book hints at the fact that we are all secret agents in the secret life of God. Indeed, the secret life of God is so secret that it is secret to most of us, who, in fact, are living it.

But it doesn't have to be. . . .

I

Living God's Secret Life

GRASPING THE TRUTH ABOUT LIFE is like watching a photograph in the midst of the developing process—first there is a little gray emerging in the corner; then something a little darker appears in the middle; little by little the shadows fill in, definitions appear, and eventually the actual images are visible. But only when the whole picture emerges can you really understand what you are seeing.

Photographs never develop in a linear or a horizontal way—it is always a little here and a little there. Truth is very much like that—if you want to grasp it, you must wait until you see the whole picture. So please be patient as you read this book. The beginning will make even more sense as you progress toward the end. However, even after you get the whole picture, you have to remember it is just a "picture" of the truth. It is not the truth itself. The picture is no more the truth than a menu is the meal. No matter how delicious the descriptions on the menu sound, you have to taste the food to know what it is.

I once saw a frustrated cat attacking a picture of a hamburger hanging in the bottom corner of the window of a restaurant. In his hunger, he had confused the picture with the food. It is important that you don't make the same mistake and confuse the picture with the truth.

The picture is only an approximation of the truth in words and concepts. To know the truth, you have to experience it. This is especially true when it comes to Kabbalah. The writings of Kabbalah are like sheet music. A person who can't read sheet music would never believe that these lines, dots, squiggles, and numbers actually express passion, harmony, and movement. Sheet music looks very technical, rigid, and mathematical. But, even though at first glance it doesn't seem to be music, it is, and only a musician knows how to translate the sheet music into song. To appreciate Kabbalah, you need to learn how to translate its sheet music into song.

There are lots of books for sale on Kabbalah and Jewish mysticism, and when you finish reading some of them (particularly the more sophisticated ones), you are indeed mystified, unable to figure out what on earth the author's talking about. But that's a false impression. Kabbalah really does make sense. It can be understood, if you remember to distinguish between the sheet music and the song, the menu and the meal, the picture of truth and the truth.

Kabbalah makes sense, but it does not always make *logical* sense to our minds, like the equation $1 + 1 = 2$. Kabbalah makes *spiritual* sense to our souls, like the equation $1 + 1 = 1$, which is the equation of love. Love makes sense, but to understand it you can't just think about it; you have to experience it.

So first we will take a look at the sheet music of Kabbalah. However, keep in mind that even the sheet music that I'm presenting is not the complete work—I cannot possibly discuss in one book all the divine melodies written for the symphony of life. So this is an abridged version—a "sketchy" picture of the truth, if you will. But even so, it will suffice in answering the deep questions that will be asked.

In this first chapter, you will discover answers to some of the most serious and challenging questions ever asked about God. But to fully understand these answers you will have to experience them in your own life.

THE QUESTIONS

* Is God perfect?
* If God is perfect, why did He create such an imperfect world and such an imperfect me?
* Can God fail, struggle with failure, and experience the ecstasy of triumph?
* Does God suffer? Can He rise to the challenge of suffering, transcend suffering, and feel pleasure?
* Does God feel sadness? Can He struggle with sadness, overcome sadness, and achieve joy?
* Can God make mistakes, regret, repent, and grow from mistakes?
* Is God absolutely good?
* If God is absolutely good, can He struggle with evil and triumphantly choose the good?
* Why did God create a world that has so much potential for evil?
* Why does God allow evil people to exist?

In answering these questions, we are going to explore some incredibly powerful ideas that reveal who is God, who are we, why we exist, and who we may become.

A NEW PICTURE

One day, as I was taking a walk in Manhattan, I suddenly became very aware of the tall skyscrapers and the hustle bustle of the thousands of people around me. It was an intimidating feeling. When I got to the street corner, the light turned red, and, as I waited, a crowd started to close in around me, making me feel squeezed and overwhelmed. All of a sudden it hit me: "I am nothing more than a fiber in this huge blob of meat, in this New York melting pot of flesh." When the light turned green, I was carried off by the massive crowds of Manhattan, feeling myself drowning in the stream of melting humanity. Just as I got to the other side of the street, I saw a flyer taped on a telephone post. In an almost unreadable scrawl, it announced:

> Come to the Cocoa Café
> and hear the GREATEST guitar player
>   in the WORLD.
> BE THERE OR BE SQUARE.

Now, that was a bit too much for me. It was hard enough to be a nothing, but to be a "square nothing" was beyond what I could handle. But more than that, I was really shocked that in the midst of this enormous world where everyone is *nothing*, there was someone who had the chutzpah, the gall, to think he is not only *something*, but the *greatest* something in the world.

And I suddenly felt that, somehow, he could be right.

Sir Arthur Eddington, the famous astrophysicist, explains that if we were to make a parallel between the universe and Grand Central Station filled to the rafters with dust, then one speck of dust would be proportionately equal to the size of planet Earth. Now, consider: if approximately six billion people live on our planetary speck of dust, then that would mean that you and I are at most one-sixth of a billionth of a speck of dust, and we are not even taking into consideration all the animals and all the trees and the minuscule creatures that inhabit our planet.

The song "Dust in the Wind" is actually very optimistic, because we are much less than dust in the wind. And yet, although scientifically I am "nothing"—how else can I put it?— deep inside I know that I am something. Somehow inside I feel that I am significant. I dare to believe that I really make a difference in this world.

So who are we? Why are we? Why did God create us? And does our existence really matter?

In answer, let me share with you a story from Kabbalah. In reading this story, keep in mind that Kabbalah does not call God "God." When Kabbalah describes the Creator of the universe, it calls Him the Ein Sof, "the Endless One." Furthermore, Kabbalah, and all other sources of Jewish wisdom, assume that God is unknowable, that we can only know those *aspects* of God that are revealed to us. Therefore, the sages speak about the *light* of God—the "Endless Light"—which is a metaphor for revelation. What we can know about God is only that which is revealed to us.

So now for our story:

When the Endless One wanted to create the world, He withdrew His Endless Light from the center, creating a spherical vacuum. In this vacuum, the Endless One created vessels and then projected a thin ray of Endless Light into the vessels. But because the vessels were unable to contain the light, they broke, and the cosmos went into a state of chaos. Kabbalah goes on to explain that life is meant to be a process of *tikkun*, meaning "repair," "fix" or "reconstruct." The vessels must be reconstructed so that they will one day succeed in holding the light. Life is all about fixing the broken vessels so that they will be able to receive the light.

Kabbalah ends this story with a paradox. It states that although the light *surrounds* the spherical vacuum, it still *fills* the vacuum. This means that the light was withdrawn and yet mysteriously continues to remain in place.

Paradox is not a problem for Kabbalah, because life does not have to fit into the neat prerequisites of logic as formulated by the Greeks. Jewish tradition does not believe that God thinks as we do nor that He created the world according to our way of thinking. Indeed, God said: "My thoughts are not like your thoughts" (Isaiah 55:8). The universe functions according to a divine supernal logic.

One of the greatest challenges to modern science has been posed by the paradoxes of the world. For instance, when it was discovered that light was both a wave and a particle, science had no choice but to question the logic of logic. For light to be both a wave and a particle was a contradiction; thus science needed to accept that reality does not always function according to our preconceived "either/or" structure. Perhaps there is another kind of logic beyond the limitations of either/or.

Indeed, science developed a new kind of logic, called quantum logic. But the Kabbalists knew quantum logic long before the scientists; they knew the theory of relativity long before Einstein. This is why the Kabbalists would never think of describing the world from God's perspective. We could not have God's perspective unless we *were* God. As noted above, what we can know about God is only that which is revealed to us, in relation to our own perception.

Incidentally, scientists make the same disclaimer. They say, "We are not describing the particle as it is, but only the way it looks to us. Therefore, light can be both a wave and a particle. Light looks different depending on the experiment we set up. *Everything* is relative to our human perspective."

With that Kabbalah agrees one hundred percent, adding: And that includes our view of God.

When we try to articulate the truth about God with our logical minds, we end up with paradoxical statements. Please remember not to confuse the menu with the meal. Although the menu is a paradox, the meal is paradise.

Is God Perfect?

In order to understand this kabbalistic story and its underlying paradoxical reasoning, we have to ask a question that will initially sound ridiculous: Is God perfect, and if so, can a perfect God become perfect?

Now, most of us would immediately answer, "If God could become perfect, that would mean that initially God was not perfect. Therefore, if He *is* perfect, He cannot *become* perfect."

But when we think about it a little more, we might ask, "If the 'Perfect One' could not become perfect, would that not be an imperfection? Would that not be a limitation? Would that mean that the perfect God could not participate in a dynamic process of growth and change from imperfect to more and more perfection? Would that mean that God lives a static, boring, unadventurous life? Is God lacking the joy in life that we have—the joy in meeting challenges and accomplishing goals?"

"Can the perfect God become perfect?" is similar to the question people sometimes ask to drive theologians crazy: Can God create a rock that He Himself cannot pick up?

Of course, if you say no, then they'll say that God is not All-Powerful. "What, He can't create a rock that He cannot pick up?"

So you say, "Oh, O.K., so then, yes, God can create such rock." But then they scoff, "You mean, He is not Almighty? He can't pick it up?"

That question pushes you into a logical corner. But Kabbalah has an answer. The answer is yes and no.

You might say, "It must be either yes or no." However, that would be demanding of God (who is the Ultimate Reality and the Source of all logic) to fit into the rigid confines of human logic. Who says the Ultimate Reality functions according to human logic? Who says that the logical human mind is constructed in a way that it can completely describe the Ultimate Reality?

Kabbalah says the answer is yes and no, because God is beyond the either/or. And therefore when we pose the question "Can the perfect become perfect?" the answer is yes and no.

In other words, when we describe the absolute perfection of God, we must describe it in a paradoxical way. Absolute perfection has the possibility for two types of perfection, which can exist simultaneously—being perfect and becoming perfect. In other words, absolute perfection includes a possibility for both a static perfection that never changes and a dynamic perfection, which is ever changing, evolving, and growing from "imperfection" to "more perfection."

ABSOLUTE PERFECTION

being perfect	becoming perfect
static perfection	dynamic perfection
never-changing	ever-changing

However, remember that this is a description relative to our limited viewpoint; from God's perspective, there is simply oneness. It is only because of the limitation of our logical minds that we describe the one God as having two types of perfection—a static perfection and a dynamic perfection; being perfect and becoming perfect.

Therefore, when *we* describe God, the Ultimate Reality, the Absolutely Perfect One, we would have to say that included within the full definition of God's absolute perfection is the possibility of becoming perfect (from imperfection toward greater and greater perfection) while being perfect.

Please notice, I am very careful with my words: I speak of a *possibility*. I do not say that God necessarily *must* become perfect, because that would be a limitation. God doesn't have to do anything. God acts freely. However, becoming perfect calls for something *to perfect*, an imperfection. Therefore, included within absolute perfection is the possibility for imperfection as the foundation of a process of becoming perfect.

Here is how it would be expressed in the language of the Kabbalah. In the beginning there was Endless Light—Absolute Perfection. When God, the Endless One, wanted to create the possibility for a process of becoming perfect, He removed His Absolute Perfection and created a vacuum, a lack, an emptiness.

Within that vacuum God created limited vessels and gave them Endless Light, even though He knew that they couldn't handle it and would break. In other words, God intentionally caused a breakdown, chaos, and imperfection. God wanted the vessels to get a taste of the perfect light even though they would break down, so that they would yearn, work, and grow toward perfection. In this way God created imperfection and set in motion a dynamic process of growth and becoming toward perfection. However, although the Endless Light surrounds this vacuum, it still fills it—and there continues to be static perfection. Therefore, mysteriously there exists simultaneously both being perfect and becoming perfect.

In summary, included within the Divine is a dynamic process at work. Within the Divine is the possibility for imperfection that grows toward perfection.

Now we can understand why you and I exist. We are the imperfect vessels. God created imperfect human beings who struggle to become better and gradually work their way toward becoming more and more perfect. We are the broken vessels, and it is through us that God fulfills His desire to express and participate in a process of becoming perfect.

You and I, who are imperfect, struggling in an imperfect world, working toward achieving more perfection, are actually necessary vehicles for the expression of the dynamic aspect of divine perfection. We are those broken vessels living in a world of chaos, but we have a memory of a perfect light, which we yearn for and strive toward. We are born in this world restless to get somewhere. We are born with a thirst for achieving the unlimited power of perfection because we have, although just for a moment, tasted it.

Absolute perfection includes the possibility for a dynamic perfection. When God chose to actualize this possibility, then you and I were created as the vehicles for the expression of this type of perfection—this aspect of Divinity. This is what's divine about our humanness. This is what's perfect about our imperfection. This is what's perfect about our constant desire and struggle to build and improve our world and ourselves.

Does God Need Us?

When I was a kid I thought that God was bored and wanted a pet to play with, since, when I was bored, I amused myself with my pet guinea pig, putting him through all sorts of interesting challenges involving mazes and obstacles that I made out of cardboard. So I thought that God did the same thing, except that I was the guinea pig.

Many adults today have a similar idea of God and creation. They think that God was floating in outer space somewhere and for some whimsical and ludicrous reason decided to create people. They will say that God didn't need to create you or me, and has no vested interest in us, but He just "felt like" creating us.

Such a perspective robs us of any intrinsic divine value. It robs us of any ultimate significance. It communicates that essentially we can do nothing for God, except perhaps amuse Him in moments of boredom; we have nothing ultimate to contribute. Our existence really doesn't matter or make a difference to God.

But that is not true. And once you understand the depths of what Kabbalah is teaching, you begin to realize how significant you are. God needs us—or, to be more accurate, God chooses to need us. God doesn't need to manifest dynamic perfection, though He is free to do so. However, once God chooses to manifest this possibility, then imperfect you and I—struggling in this imperfect world in a process of becoming, striving toward perfection—are necessary to God. This is what Jewish tradition means when it teaches that the work of humanity is of lofty necessity to God.

It's been said that happiness is the certainty of being needed. If you feel that you are completely disposable and unnecessary, if you think that nobody needs you, then you're not going to be happy. Human beings need to feel needed. And that is because we are.

Kabbalah reveals that God chooses to need us. Our humanness, our imperfection and struggle toward becoming perfect, are necessary and meaningful to God as part of God's desire to express and participate in this type of perfection—"becoming perfect."

WHY DID GOD CREATE THIS IMPERFECT WORLD?

If God is perfect, then why did He create such an imperfect world filled with imperfect people?

The very first verse of the Book of Genesis tells us: "In the beginning God created heaven and earth, and earth was in a state of chaos." This sounds like God did a pretty crummy job. The minute He creates the world, it's already in a state of chaos.

But the truth is that God did a perfect job. What's perfect about this world *is* the chaos! It's the perfect place for growth. It's the perfect place for challenge. It's the perfect setting for triumph. It is the perfect stage for an exciting drama about becoming perfect.

If you struggle with the chaos within you and around you and turn it into order, then you are doing a great divine service. If you acknowledge your imperfections and the imperfections of this world, work hard, and rise to the challenge to fix them, then you are a vehicle for the expression of God's dynamic perfection.

This is our human greatness. This is our mission on earth and service to God. We are human characters in a divine drama.

"Nobody's perfect" is precisely what's so perfect about everybody. However, this is true only when you use your imperfections as starting points for growth. If you don't, then you are not part of the divine process and God is not part of your life. You have forfeited the very meaning and value of your existence.

This world is meant to be difficult, and your life on earth is meant to be a struggle, filled with adventure, challenge, and victory. This is your divine mission if you are willing to accept it. And if you accept it, you will have the power to succeed.

Why did God create an imperfect world filled with imperfect people? Because God's absolute perfection includes the possibility for dynamic perfection—becoming perfect. This type of perfection is expressed through imperfect you and me, struggling in this imperfect world to improve ourselves and this world, striving and working hard toward becoming perfect.

CAN GOD FAIL?

If God is perfect, does He lack the ability to fail, struggle, and be triumphant?

Would you want a life without the possibility of failure? Could you really win if you could never fail? Would you want to play a football game against a team of five-year-olds when you know for sure you'd win? What fun is that?

You want to play a game that is more challenging. You want to play a game that you know there is a chance you will lose, but you want to fight until you win. If there is no possibility of losing, then there is no possibility of winning. Indeed, there would be no adventure and no fun to the game. There really is no game. Players often come back from a hard game, bruised, limping, and yet praising, "What a great game!"

We all love the challenge, the possibility of failure, the opportunity to struggle, and the ecstasy of victory.

Is it possible that God lacks this? No! God participates in all this through you and me. God created the human being and invested in that imperfect being an aspect of the divine self—the soul. The Jewish tradition metaphorically describes the soul, the real you, as a spark of God.

I often wondered, "What's a spark of the perfect God doing in an imperfect character like me, and in an imperfect world like this?"

The Kabbalah gave me the answer: "That's what's so great

about you—that you're not so great! And that's what's so perfect about you—that you're not so perfect!"

The human enterprise is an essential vehicle for the expression of divine dynamic perfection. God's absolute perfection includes the possibility for simultaneously being perfect and becoming perfect. The light surrounds the vacuum. There is a vacuum. There is emptiness and there is lack. There is deficiency and breakdown. There are problems and there is a mess. And therefore there's an opportunity for change, struggle, adventure, challenge, creativity, and excitement. This is the exciting game of life.

God does not lack participation in failure, struggle, and triumph, because He invested a spark of His Divinity in the human being—an imperfect character living in this difficult and challenging world. God lives in this world and partakes in the challenge and adventure of becoming perfect through you and me. This does not mean that we are God. But it does mean that we are an aspect of God—you and I are sparks of God. And this we must always remember, that although God is manifest within us, He continues to be beyond us.

DOES GOD SUFFER?

What would life be like if there was no suffering? Would there be pleasure? Imagine if you were rich, your friends were rich, and you lived in an entirely rich neighborhood. And let's say you lived a very sheltered life and never saw one magazine, newspaper, or movie that dealt with the topic of poverty. Would you be rich if you'd never experienced or heard of poverty?

Kirk Douglas, the legendary actor, once told me, "I gave my children everything but one gift I couldn't give them, the gift of poverty." Kirk grew up in a poverty-stricken home. There were nine members in his family, and sometimes all they had was only one egg.

A couple of years ago a woman registered for one of my seminars at Isralight, the spiritual retreat center that I founded.

She was one of the most amazing people I had ever met. She was radiant with the joy of life.

I said to her, "You are a remarkable person; you're really beaming with light." She responded, "Oh, Rabbi, I can tell you why." She pulled up her sleeve and showed me scars running down her arm. Then she showed me her other arm, also filled with scars.

She said, "Rabbi, I have scars all over my body. About five years ago I was in a car accident. My friend was at the wheel and lost control of the car, and it went over a cliff. The car rolled over a number of times and finally came to a halt. In that moment, I realized that I was still conscious, I was still alive. I pulled myself out of the car, but then I saw that my friend was wedged into the wreck. So I ran back to pull her out. At that point the car exploded. And I exploded with the car. The ambulance came and took me to the hospital. I was put into rehabilitation for about a year and a half, to relearn the basic motor skills of life. Rabbi, I have to tell you, that it was the greatest gift of my life. My radiance and happiness did not come without much pain and work."

Many of the great leaders who have impacted upon civilization had very difficult lives. Their strength of character, drive, and determination rarely came without a high price of challenge, pain, and struggle. Their lives were a roller-coaster, not a merry-go-round. Most of them would admit that their zeal for life, intellectual depth, idealistic vision, and commitment came from much anguish and conflict.

I once addressed a group of people in Miami who had suffered much damage from Hurricane Andrew. The class was titled "Serenity and Suffering," and it was held in a home that was hit badly by the 1992 hurricane. You could see that the attendees were still devastated by the horrifying experience they had gone through. I asked them how they were feeling, and I was shocked by their response:

"It was so amazing! We felt so much love for each other—like we never felt before. We will forever cherish the awesome feelings of unity, compassion, and sensitivity that emerged during those frightening times. Although we experienced very painful moments, there were so many precious feelings and realizations that we achieved precisely because of those painful moments."

Does God experience these great pleasures of life that come only through the challenges and difficulties of life on earth? Does God suffer, struggle with suffering, transcend suffering, and experience the pleasure of triumph?

Yes, through you and me!

If you read the personal accounts of Holocaust survivors, you will find that each and every one of them is a masterpiece. I fully understand why Steven Spielberg invested millions of dollars toward the creation of a Holocaust archive collecting every testimony possible. As a producer and a director, he understands that every single one of those stories is Oscar-winning (though I'm sure he's not doing it to win any Oscars). These reports are the epic dramas of hearts and souls, of people who in their struggles achieved beautiful qualities of love, care, integrity, trust, hope, courage—the list is endless.

Yes, there were failures. Not always did these horrifying scenes bring out the best in everyone. Yes, there were many tragic endings. But that's the price. The price for good is the possibility for evil, the price for love is the possibility for hatred, the price for happiness is the possibility for sadness, and the price for victory is the possibility for failure.

Can God pay the price, rise to these challenges that only life on earth provides, and achieve goodness, love, happiness, and victory?

Yes, through you and me.

And we can experience that ecstatic truth when we invite God into our daily struggles by praying and by rising to the challenges and improving this world and ourselves for God's sake. This is the true meaning of serving God. This is what we can do for God.

Life is a divine drama. The theme of the drama of life is

all about challenge, choices, growth, and love. It's all about the journey. We—with all our problems and complexities—are the stars of the show. The ideal setting is this messed-up world. Our true inner self, however, is none other than the soul—a spark of God.

Our mission is to accept the challenge and turn it into a service to God. Our deepest fulfillment and ultimate meaning comes from the knowledge that God needs us and joins us in order to participate in a dynamic and challenging process of becoming perfect.

God lives His secret life through you and me, if we let Him in.

Does God Feel Sadness?

Many years ago, when I returned from a trip to Israel, my parents picked me up at the airport and sadly told me that we were going to the funeral of my cousin, who had been killed in a car accident. At the funeral, the rabbi said something that angered me very much and challenged my faith in God. In his eulogy, the rabbi quoted a Yiddish saying: "What do we know? People try to figure it out, and God is laughing."

The rabbi seemed to be saying that it's only from our perspective that terrible accidents look terrible. We see the back of the tapestry of life, and it looks to us like random strands of knotted wool. God, however, sees the whole beautiful picture on the right side of the tapestry, and He's laughing because everything is in order, everything makes sense.

But the rabbi's words really upset me. Bully for God that He knows it all. But what about us? I felt like we were stupid little mice scurrying around in pain and fear, trying to find our way through a maze, while God was laughing. I didn't like that image of God at all. It only confirmed my childhood ideas, which I had been working so hard to get rid of.

But I completely misunderstood. It seemed to me as if the rabbi was saying that God is transcendent and completely removed from our pain and sadness in this world. But that's not true. Yes, the Torah and Kabbalah teach that God is transcendent, "outside" the world, a perfect *being*. But the Torah and Kabbalah also teach that God is imminent, "inside" this world, and manifest as a perfect *becoming*—the very soul of humanity, completely immersed in our ups and downs, our happy times and our sad times.

A story is told about a businessman whose company purchased a coal mine. However, shortly after the sale, the price of coal began to drop in response to the fluctuation in fossil fuels. Distressed by the financial loss, the man went to get advice from a Kabbalist. The sage told him, "The Talmud says that when a person is in distress this causes the Shekhinah, God's Presence in the world, also to feel anguish. If you are in pain over your financial loss, this causes God to suffer along with you. So what do you think? Is it worthwhile causing God to be saddened over a few pieces of coal?"

Life is difficult. But then again, it depends on how you look at it. I once watched my kids take hundreds of pieces of a puzzle and spend long, hard hours putting it together. I had planned to frame it once it was finished, but they had a different idea. They celebrated its completion by destroying it. Why? Because they were not interested in the puzzle's being completed! They were interested in the excitement of doing the puzzle, the challenge and adventure of making it. That's what they enjoyed about it.

They understood what we should all understand. There's so much life and value in the process, so much growth and awareness in the journey, as difficult as it may sometimes be.

Kabbalah teaches us that God takes the journey with us. God is intimately involved in our daily challenges and struggles, in our ups and downs. God shares our pains and troubles as well as our pleasures and successes. Knowing this makes difficult experiences more manageable and more meaningful. Knowing this also makes the good times even better. I have heard it said that when you share your sadness with another person it is halved, and when you share your joy it is doubled. This is all the more so when you realize that God shares in your sadness and joys.

We are all here for the journey. However, we get the most out of our journey when we turn it into a holy journey by acknowledging that God is with us.

CAN GOD MAKE MISTAKES?

Can God make mistakes, regret, repent, and experience the joy in growing from mistakes?

Yes, through you and me.

It's important to understand that the theme of life is *teshuvah*. Most commonly translated as "repentance," *teshuvah* has nothing to do with undergoing penance (as in sackcloth and ashes); it means literally "to return" and describes specifically the intricate process of returning to God, returning to a life of growth and dynamic perfection, accepting anew the opportunity for serving God.

This intricate process begins with fixing one's mistakes and resolving not to repeat them, but it's more than that.

Kabbalah teaches that *teshuvah* is the theme of the cosmos. God intentionally set in motion the breaking of the vessels. He intentionally created a world full of chaos so that there would be an opportunity for challenge, which would create the possibility of error. Having made mistakes, we can then experience remorse and struggle to find the courage to change for the better. We can then humble ourselves to ask forgiveness and commit ourselves to continued growth.

Therefore, *teshuvah* isn't relevant exclusively to individuals and their mistakes. Whatever one does affects the entire cosmos, because everything that happens works toward the making of order out of the chaos and contributes to the process of becoming perfect.

Teshuvah is actually the theme of life. We are always in the midst of *teshuvah*. Life is an endless journey—an adventure in becoming. It's all about improving, building, and accomplishing—that's what we love doing.

It doesn't always seem so wonderful. But if it did, there would be no growth. We would miss the opportunity to make mistakes, grow from them, celebrate the triumph, and experience the sweetness of forgiveness.

God put you in this world (which is one great obstacle course) but also joins you in the challenge.

God is like a great coach who's training you for the Olympics. He sets up a training ground filled with obstacles. That is His gift to you. He is really creating opportunities for you to jump higher. He also knows that the higher you need to jump, the harder you could fall. But that's the price you pay to enter the Olympics. You are bound to make mistakes and fail sometimes. But when you do, don't despair. It's all part of the process. Just try again, and keep moving forward. Don't spend your valuable time beating yourself up over the past, constantly bemoaning all the mistakes you made. Jewish tradition reminds us that great people make great mistakes.

Of course, you must recognize that you made a mistake, and you should regret it and resolve never to do it again. But don't think that you will never make another mistake. In fact, expect that it's bound to happen, and no human being is exempt from this.

This is part of our service to God, the aspect of absolute divine perfection that we express. However, we need to remember the profound mystery that God is not only our coach urging us to greater achievements, but is also the source of the runner (the soul) within us. And He has a vested interest in the outcome of the race.

Sometime ago I read a book called *I'm O.K., You're O.K.* After I read it, I felt O.K. but not great. Maybe I misunderstood the book, but I took it to mean "Nobody's perfect." Everybody makes mistakes. So just accept that they are O.K., that's O.K., and you're O.K.

Torah and Kabbalah don't want you to think you are O.K.

They want you to know that you are great. Their message is "I'm Great, You're Great." We are all manifestations of God's greatness in this world. We are vehicles for the expression of one type of divine perfection—dynamic perfection. Through you and me God fulfills His desire to participate in the process of *teshuvah*, making mistakes and growing from them.

We are not just O.K. We are great. And part of our greatness is the possibility to make mistakes, stumble, and fall sometimes. It's not that we *want* to fall or *try* to fall. But sometimes we do make mistakes. No matter how low we fall—even when we intentionally commit horrible crimes—we can always recycle our garbage into the gold of growth and dynamic perfection.

When we realize this, we will be able to forgive ourselves and we will recognize how much God forgives us. God knew when He created this world of chaos that the stakes were very high. He created a world that offers the greatest opportunity for an adventure in becoming perfect. Here is the greatest opportunity for mistakes, yet the greatest opportunity for change and forgiveness. Here is the greatest opportunity for hate, but also the greatest opportunity for love. Here is the greatest opportunity for cruelty, but also the greatest opportunity for kindness.

God knew the stakes were high. Therefore, God forgives us when we make those mistakes, if we are genuine in our recognition of them and work hard to change.

The Talmud, the compilation of Jewish oral tradition, suggests that God also wants our forgiveness. How is this possible?

I have a very loving dentist, and as he drills away at my tooth, he constantly asks me to forgive him for the pain he is causing me. And although everything he is doing is only for my good, it's possible for me to forget that at times and feel angry. And so, too, in this sometimes painful and challenging life of becoming perfect, it's important, for our own sakes, to forgive God—even though deep down we intuit that everything that happens is an expression of ultimate goodness. The opportunity to serve God and be a vehicle for His process of becoming perfect is the very gift of life.

Is God Absolutely Good?

Is God good? Can God choose goodness?

Goodness that isn't chosen is not complete goodness. If we didn't choose goodness—if we were just naturally good, or if goodness was the only option available—how could that be the highest expression of goodness?

I know a fellow that has dozens of guests over at his home every weekend. When I complimented him on his hospitality, he said, "What are you talking about? It comes naturally to me. It's not a struggle for me. I love to do this!"

Is he really choosing goodness? If it comes naturally, is it complete goodness? Goodness that wasn't chosen is not the greatest good. Only after you struggle with evil and chose goodness will you accomplish true and complete goodness.

Does God struggle with evil? Can God experience complete goodness through overcoming evil and choosing the good?

Yes, through you and me. God participates in complete goodness through our choices.

Our service to God is to choose goodness. That's why we're in a world so full of allurements to do evil—so that we can rise to the challenge and choose good. That's our service to God. God needs us to choose good. For there to be choice, evil has to be pretty attractive. There is no choice if we're not interested in one of the alternatives. In other words, if somebody puts in front of me a gorgeous, delicious meal, and next to it a plate of (forgive me) vomit, would it be a tremendous choice that I opted for the meal and not the vomit?

Therefore, in order for there to be the optimal opportunity to choose goodness, evil has to be extremely attractive. People think the Devil is an independent character who has a red ugly face, horns on his head, and a pitchfork in his hand. Kabbalah teaches that the forces of evil were created by God and the strongest ones are a counterfeit of good. They look just like goodness. That's why they present such a great challenge. Evil and good are not always like black and white. High-grade, superclassy evil looks just like good, but it's counterfeit nevertheless. Counterfeit means that it looks like the real thing but isn't.

I walk into a store. I hand the cashier a bill. The cashier says, "Thank you, sir. Oh, wait a second! . . . Sir, I'm sorry, this hundred-dollar bill is worthless; it's counterfeit."

I then begin to argue, "What are you talking about? This is a hundred-dollar bill! Do you see the number 100 in the corner?"

The cashier shrugs. "No, I'm sorry, sir, this bill is a worthless piece of paper. President Washington's right eyeball is slightly off."

"No, no, this is one hundred dollars. What's an eyeball got to do with it?"

"Sir, just because it looks, smells, and feels like a hundred-dollar bill doesn't make it a hundred-dollar bill. Unless it's printed at the U.S. Mint, it's worthless."

So, too, the choices for goodness in real life are often much more subtle than most people recognize. There is a subtle but real difference between "looking good" and "being good."

Torah and Kabbalah teach that God created the world in order to facilitate the possibility for ultimate goodness, which means goodness that has been chosen. Our service to God is to choose goodness.

Life is all about choices. There are always choices to be made. Every day we are all handed choices. Every day we all get different challenges. No one can expect life to be a piece of cake in a world of choices.

But don't worry. Try your best, and if you make a mistake, you can do *teshuvah*. You can be forgiven. Remember, God knew the stakes were high, and God is with you in your pain and struggle.

In fact, the Talmud tells us that before God created the world, He created the power of *teshuvah*, because the likelihood of our making mistakes was so great that we couldn't even last a moment without the possibility of *teshuvah* already available.

Teshuvah is amazing. The Talmud teaches that if we transgress but later on change because we fear punishment, then our offense is considered null and void. But if we transgress but later on mend our ways because of our love for God, then our offense is counted as a merit in the spiritual realm.

Imagine a person who spent their whole life choosing evil and darkness. But moments before they die, they do *teshuvah* for the love of God. They are able to take all their offenses and turn them into merits and light. How is this possible?

When we do *teshuvah* out of fear, it means we're afraid of the pain that is the likely consequence of our choices. When fear motivates our personal transformation, it is because we want to protect ourselves. And that's a noble move.

However, when we do *teshuvah* out of our love for God, the underlying motivation is that we acknowledge the pain and disappointment we have caused God. We realize that God was counting on us to beat evil and choose good, and we failed Him. And we are so sorry for the missed opportunity to reveal this great goodness born out of choice.

Teshuvah done out of love arises from the realization that we are here on earth to perform a divine service—to choose goodness for God's sake. God wants to participate in complete goodness through our struggle against evil and our choice to do the good, but we have failed Him. We do *teshuvah* not because we fear punishment but because we love God and know that we have, so to speak, let God down. This realization itself brings us closer to God, even closer than we were before we made the mistakes. Therefore, all our offenses turn into merits. The darkness is converted into light.

If God is absolutely good, why did He create a world that has so much evil?

Ultimate goodness, which is the goodness achieved through choice, requires the possibility for evil. Once you understand this, you will appreciate how central a role evil plays in this world. What's so good about this world is the evil in it. This world offers the opportunity to beat evil and choose good.

In other words, Kabbalah is teaching that the main feature and advantage of this world is the evil in it. This world was not created for what is already good in it. This world was created to be a forum for a new and higher kind of goodness—the goodness born out of overcoming evil and choosing to do good.

Imagine you walk into a factory and you see them trucking in tons and tons of garbage. You then find out that they actually buy this garbage and that it is their most valued raw material. This all sounds crazy to you until you find out that this factory is actually a recycling plant. They take garbage and turn it into usable products. Welcome to World, Inc.!

Yes, this world is really a recycling plant. This is why it is filled with so much garbage. All the trash around us and within us is here for us to recycle into usable products—lessons and realizations, growth and accomplishments. Before I learned this lesson from Kabbalah, I always wondered why there was so much evil in the world. However, after this secret was revealed to me, I asked: Why isn't there more evil in this world? The answer, of course, is that there is less evil because we are working so hard and succeeding in our mission on earth to choose good.

WE ARE NOT ALONE

No tear ever shed in the history of humanity is without divine participation. We are never alone, although we can choose to forget that truth by kicking God out of our awareness, out of our struggles and challenges.

When we pray to God, we are not simply saying, "God, remove all these problems and make everything easy. Snap Your cosmic fingers and make it all better." When we pray to God, we're actually consciously inviting God into our struggle. In this way we empower ourselves to fulfill our mission in the world.

I think this is one of the most important ideas of Torah and Kabbalah: we're not alone in our struggle, in our challenges, in our pain. God is always with us. God is rooting for us all the time.

In Kabbalah the forces of evil are called *sitra acher*, "the other side." One of the tricks of evil is to try to convince you that God is on the other side. You're on one side and God is on the other side. He's not on your side. He is against you.

This is a lie. God is always on your side. No matter how low you feel you have fallen, God is always on your side. To feel this, all you have to do is invite Him in.

A child once asked his father, where is God? His father responded, "Wherever you let Him in."

The teachings of the Torah and Kabbalah focus on letting God into your process, inviting God into your challenge, and recognizing how much God wants to be involved and is involved in your life, because your true inner self is the soul, a spark of God.

Therefore, we are incredibly important to God. And God is always with us. If we don't choose to believe that, then—although we are important to God and He is always with us just the same—we won't experience the joy of that truth.

In Summary

God is not out to get you. God is not on another side. God is always on your side. God has a vested interest in you—because you are a soul, a spark of Himself. You are not God, but you are a spark of God. Although God is beyond you, an aspect of God is manifest within you. Every situation you're in, God orchestrates to maximize your possibility to choose goodness, growth, and achievement.

God is not some magician who casually snapped his finger and created us with no vested interest in what would happen to us. God is not some force removed from our process, pain, and struggle, stoically looking down at us while we grapple with life in this world.

According to Torah and Kabbalah, God, who is loving and caring, created you and me in this world as a vehicle for the expression of the full possibility of Himself—His absolute perfection.

God's absolute perfection, as described from our limited human perspective, has two facets: static perfection (being perfect) and dynamic perfection (becoming perfect). Through you and me, God fulfills His desire to express and participate in a challenging and adventurous process of becoming perfect.

When you realize that you are part of God's life and God is part of your life, you will discover your holiness, your ultimate meaning and significance. When you realize that you exist within the Endless Light of God, you will discover that God's Endless Light is also inside of you. You will understand that an aspect of God's absolute perfection—the dynamic perfection—is expressed through you. Your divine privilege is to be a human being who serves as a vehicle for God. When you serve the ultimate, then you're part of the ultimate. When you realize that you're part of the ultimate, then you experience the perfection of every moment.

Here's the menu put simply: God is living His secret life through you.

Take a moment to contemplate, feel, and taste this delicious truth. Take a lifetime to live it and celebrate it.

2

Your Divine Mission

FOR A BETTER UNDERSTANDING of what we have been discussing, I would like to examine a strange story related in the Talmud. The sages encoded very deep ideas in stories such as this one, which is highly allegorical and not meant to be taken literally.

The point of the story, as will soon be clear, is to explain who we are and what God wants from us on earth.

I will retell the highlights here, though using a more contemporary style, forgoing Talmudic terminology and simplifying the language. And I will weave into the story the philosophical message it is intended to communicate.

As the story begins, the angels are all excited because God has brought out a special treasure—the Ten Commandments—from His storehouse. The angels know that encoded in these commandments is a special mission from God, and since angels are the agents of God carrying out all His missions, they can't wait to find out which one of them will get this choice assignment.

Just then, to their great surprise, huffing and puffing up the mountain scrambles an old man, who, when he introduces himself at the gates of heaven, has a bad stutter. This, of course, is Moses. The angels are aghast. "Master of the Universe," they say to God, "what is this imperfect earthling doing among us perfect heavenly creatures? What business does he have to be up here in the angelic realm?"

"Don't worry," God reassures them. "He is not staying up here. He just came to pick up the Ten Commandments."

The angels didn't find that calming at all. "What? You've been holding on to this treasured assignment for 974 generations. And now You're going to give it to a mortal man? What are his qualifications that You would entrust him with a heavenly mission like this? He'll just take it down to earth to be desecrated. Don't give it to him—give it to us!"

And God says to Moses, "You have to answer them. You must refute their objection."

Why doesn't God refute the angels' objection? Because God is telling Moses, "You can't get this treasured assignment unless you know why you're getting it. No one can answer these questions for you. You have to find the confidence and courage within yourself to claim your worthiness. You must understand what your qualifications are as a human being to receive this great honor; because when you accept the commandments of God, it means you are accepting a divine mission: you become God's agent."

SECRET AGENT

To be God's agent is an awesome responsibility. If you appoint someone to be your agent, he or she is equal to yourself. You have given that person your power of attorney, to act on your behalf.

This is what the commandments are: a statement of the mission to be performed on God's behalf by us human beings on earth. When you accept the mission of the commandments, you become God's agent on earth just as angels are God's agents in heaven. That's why Moses had to go to the angelic realm to get the treasure and bring it to earth.

The angels don't know the details of this mission; all they know is that it must really be important to God if He has been holding on to it for so long and has not yet appointed anyone to do it. But a human being? This is absurd!

From the viewpoint of the angels, human beings are such lowly creatures, filled with base inclinations. How can they be entrusted with something so holy? How is it possible that this imperfect being could ascend beyond the power of the angels and fulfill this Godly treasured assignment in a messed-up place like earth?

God says to Moses, "You have to respond to these angels' complaints. You have to understand why you deserve this mission. Explain to them your qualifications."

Most people think that the commandments are all about believing in God. But that's only half the story. The message encoded in the commandments is also about believing in yourself. To accept the commandments, you must believe that you have the power to serve God. You are worthy to be God's agent on earth and fulfill a sacred mission. This requires a tremendous amount of self-confidence and self-esteem. You can do something for God. You can represent God on earth because He has entrusted you with His power of attorney.

This view is at odds with the view that has dominated Western culture—that of the Greeks. The Greeks believed that the gods were so great that it was beneath their divine dignity to bother with human beings. "Human affairs are hardly worth considering in earnest, and yet we must be earnest about them—a sad necessity constrains us," says Plato (*Laws*, VII, 803). And according to Aristotle, the gods are not concerned with the dispensation of good and bad fortune or external things (*Magna Moralia*, II, 8, 1207–9). The Roman statesman Cicero taught that "the gods attend to great matters; they neglect small ones" (*De Natura Deorum*, II, 167).

But from the commandments we understand that God is so great that He even cares about little you and me and the little things we do. This itself is God's greatness. The Torah's message is that you are really important, significant, and powerful. You have been given the might to represent the Almighty. You have been entrusted with God's power of attorney to grow, overcome evil, choose goodness, and build and improve the world on His behalf.

KNOW YOUR GREATNESS

The story continues:

God says to Moses, "I cannot answer for you, and, unless you realize for yourself what your qualifications are, you can't get this treasured assignment."

Moses starts to tremble. "Master of the Universe, I am afraid that I cannot compete with the angels. I am nothing compared with them."

God gives Moses a tip. "Moses, you're right! In and of yourself, you are nothing. The source of your self-worth can only come from being My servant and My agent."

With that Moses is charged with amazing confidence to face the angels. In their presence he asks God, "What's contained in the Ten Commandments?"

God responds, "It states, *I am the Lord your God, who brought you out of the land of Egypt, out of the house of bondage.*"

Moses then challenges the angels: "Did you spend 210 years in Egypt? Do you know what it means to suffer as a slave—to do humiliating, backbreaking work, being whipped by cruel taskmasters? What relevance do these words have to you?"

The angels admit that they have only lived a perfect, blissful life in heaven.

Moses continues to build his case: "God, what else is in the Ten Commandments?"

God answers, *"Thou shalt not have other gods."*

Moses confronts the angels. "Are you living among nations who worship idols?"

To really understand Moses's point, you need to appreciate what idolatry was all about. Idolatry was a lot of fun. Most forms of idolatrous practices revolved around sexual promiscuity. The idolaters believed that orgies were a service to their gods. Idolatry wasn't really about bowing down to rocks and trees. Idolators deified nature. This means that whatever happens naturally is great. If you feel an urge to do anything at all, that's fine, as you're only being true to your natural self—and that's considered healthy and good. Now you can understand the appeal and danger of this philosophy.

Moses's point to the angels was, "Do you live in a society that challenges you daily with constant allurements and seductions?"

The angels answer, "Nahh, we're angels!"

Moses continues, "God, what else is in the Ten Commandments?"

"Keep the Sabbath. Honor thy mother and thy father. Don't murder. Don't commit adultery. Don't steal."

Moses asks, "Angels, do you work hard? Do you need rest? Do you have fathers and mothers whom you honor? Does jealousy exist among you? Do you have negative and destructive inclinations?"

The angels are stymied.

These are the qualifications Moses presented to show why humanity deserves to get the mission of the Ten Commandments.

In effect, Moses's argument was: "We humans are not perfect angels, we are lowly, imperfect beings. We struggle with evil urges all the time. We live in a materialistic society filled with daily seductions. Therefore, we should get God's mission! We qualify for this mission because we are able to make so many mistakes. We are inundated with problems and challenges from within and without. We are perfect for this job because we are so imperfect!"

The angels are impressed with this argument, and they acquiesce. The story ends with their words of praise: "Holy One, Blessed Be He! O Lord, how excellent is Your name in all the earth!"

They are so convinced that they even decide to befriend humanity and give Moses useful tips to help humanity in its challenging and difficult mission.

PERFECTLY IMPERFECT

God created humanity to be His vehicle for the expression of dynamic perfection and to participate in the struggle to become perfect. We are highly qualified for this mission because we are imperfect characters living in an imperfect world. We have an evil inclination that challenges us daily. We have the capacity to do great evil, but we can also choose to do great good. We are able to fail but also to succeed. We are able to destroy but also to build. Our lives can be filled with challenge, adventure, and growth.

Angels are perfect—they have no evil inclination, they have no free choice, they can't struggle, they can't fail. They do not wrestle to overcome evil. Only human beings can fulfill this divine mission because we are imperfect characters struggling to improve ourselves; striving to become perfect. Only human beings can fight evil, overcome evil, choose goodness, and grow. This is our divine mission, if we are willing to accept it. This is our service to God.

Angels blissfully sing God's praises in a perfect heavenly realm. However, our songs of praise surpass those of the angels, because we've got good reasons *not* to sing as we struggle with our problems, pains, and challenges here on earth.

The Talmud teaches that you don't ultimately succeed until you have first failed. In other words, part of our divine mission is to fail, regret it, resolve to change, choose goodness, and succeed. In fact, sometimes God orchestrates a situation for us to fail so that we can get to an even higher place once we fix our mistake.

Ecclesiastes (7:20) teaches, "There is no holy person in the world that does good and does not transgress." To err is human. Note that the verse specifies "in the world," because if you got out of this world, you could be perfect. If you lived on some desert island completely removed from society, then you would never hurt anyone's feelings, never get into an argument, never get jealous, and possibly never make a mistake.

But you don't and you can't, though people try.

Some people turn to religion thinking that it is a refuge from the turbulence of life, from doubt, from inner conflicts and mental turmoil. They look to religion to provide them with instant inner peace, spiritual contentment, and tranquility for their troubled souls.

According to Kabbalah, that is not the purpose of life on earth. In fact, it is just the opposite. We have been dropped right in the middle of the stormy seas of daily living. We are confronted with the problems of the world and commanded to fix them and ourselves. The commandments not only show us the work that has to be done, they actually create more problems than we had before.

The Talmud teaches that it's part of human nature that every commandment we get stirs up within us a desire to rebel. As soon as we discover that we are not allowed to do something, or we are supposed to do something, there emerges within us an inclination and desire to do just the opposite. That's one of the golden problems of being human—being stubborn, being difficult, and being complex. Therefore, the commandments do not simplify life, they actually make it more difficult.

However, when you understand that the theme of life is precisely rising to the challenges, then you can appreciate how the challenges raise the ante in the game. Remember, it is the rules of a game that make it a game at all. Imagine if football or baseball had no rules, no out-of-bounds, no fouls. Although the rules make it more challenging, they also make it more fun and ultimately more fulfilling when you win.

DIVINE SHAREHOLDERS

When the angels understood this about God's treasured assignment, they wanted a piece of the action. So they gave humanity gifts—useful secrets—in order to invest in the human enterprise. They wanted to be shareholders in Human Becomings, Inc. If you can't work for the company, at least invest in it and enjoy dividends as a shareholder.

God is the largest shareholder of the company. He is the major investor in Human Becomings, Inc. God invested a spark of the Divine Self—the soul—in human beings in order to be a participant in this world. Kabbalah teaches that God desires to be in this world. God lives and participates in this world through you and me. We experience and enjoy this honor only if we invite God into our world by accepting our challenging lives as His divine mission.

Every human being has the potential to be God's rep and agent. Everything we do can be for God's sake. This is the greatest honor and pleasure a person can experience. To live for yourself does not provide ultimate fulfillment and happiness. But when you make yourself into an instrument for God and make choices for God's sake—then you experience heaven on earth.

I sometimes ask my students at Isralight to imagine how they would reason and act if they were buying a car for God's sake. What would be the main considerations in the choice of models? Typically, they immediately dismiss appearance and the brand name of the car—they don't care if it's red, if it's a Ferrari, if it's got a turbo engine. What matters is safety features, pollution controls, mileage to the gallon, and value for the dollar. In other words, the overriding concerns are for the life of the passengers, for the environment, for conserving precious resources, for making sound economic judgments.

The next time you're about to make a decision ask yourself, "If I do this for God, what would be the right choice? If I am His rep on earth, how should I behave?"

This is the true path of responsibility. In everything we do, we should feel a responsibility to God. Don't worry—the responsibility of being an agent for God doesn't make you neurotic. It gives you great inspiration, clarity, and vitality.

LIFE IS A MISSION

Life is a mission. If you don't understand this, then your life adds up to a collection of moments and events that are disconnected from each other, leading nowhere.

Your mission is your meaning.

If you knew the definition of individual words but you didn't know how to turn those words into sentences and to turn those sentences into paragraphs, you would not have a meaningful story. If you don't know how the events of your life connect to a greater purpose and serve a greater context, then there is no sense to the story of your life.

"Life is a mission" is not just an interesting phrase. It is the key that opens up the treasures of the Torah and Kabbalah, the meaning of all the commandments, the meaning of our lives, and the joys of serving God.

I recall a cute comic strip depicting Moses coming down from Mount Sinai with the Ten Commandments written in stone. "I've got good news and bad news," he announces to the Israelites waiting anxiously at the bottom of the mountain. "The good news is that I got Him down to ten." The crowd cheers. "The bad news is that adultery is still in."

It is not uncommon for people to think the commandments spoil the fun of life—that God is really a cosmic party pooper, and that there is a conflict of interest between us and God.

People think that serving God is demeaning; servitude implies a slave-master relationship. But that is not the real meaning of serving God. The opportunity to serve God is the greatest gift we could ever imagine. It's empowering. To serve God means that we can do something on behalf of God. It's an unbelievable honor!

The Talmud teaches that if you come close to fire, you will be warm, and that the servant who comes close to the king partakes in royalty.

I've been at the home of some very, very wealthy people. I always find it so interesting that the various workers in the home—gardeners, caterers, hairdressers, and so on—live in the mansion with their boss, eat the same food, and enjoy the use of the same facilities like the pool, sauna, and Jacuzzi during their breaks.

The servants in the palace in many ways enjoy the life of royalty. And they are privy to seeing the king in private moments. They even see the king in his pajamas. They come the closest and thereby enjoy the most intimate encounters with the king.

Working for God is not a diminishing experience. On the contrary, it's the greatest elevation of status. If I build my business for my own sake, to make money for *me*, it is really nothing special. But if I build my business for God's sake, if I look at what I do and ask myself how can I promote God's purpose in this world—how can I bring more love, peace, kindness, justice, and wisdom into the world, how can I be an instrument serving to reveal divine qualities and ideals in the world—it's an unbelievable opportunity! This is the secret to a profoundly meaningful and fulfilling life.

There's a striking line in a song by Bob Dylan: "You're gonna have to serve somebody." Everybody's serving somebody. There's nobody in this world that isn't serving something or somebody else. The question is not "To serve or not to serve?" The question is "*Whom* to serve?"

If my life is dedicated to gaining approval from certain people, then I am always less than they are. But if my life is dedicated to God, then the sky's the limit to my self-worth. There is no greater mission waiting for me. There is nothing higher.

My mission on earth is not about making a lot of money. If it is, then the T-shirt slogan is right: "The one who dies with the most toys wins." But Kabbalah teaches that we have come to this world to perform the ultimate mission—a mission that elevates and brings sacredness to all of life. Life without a mission is no life at all. A person who wakes up in the morning and has nothing pressing to do will wonder after a while, "Do I really make a difference? Does my life really matter?"

FINDING YOUR MISSION

Now we have a better appreciation of the statement in the Book of Genesis that the human being was created in the image of God. As God's representative, we are a human "re-presentation" of the Divine on earth. As such, our job is to contribute to the creation of ourselves, to improve this world, to rise to the challenges, to choose goodness and grow. This is what we can do on God's behalf, for God's sake.

All human beings have been given a mission. There is a universal mission that we are all obligated in. However, there is also a unique mission for every nation—the United States, England, China, Israel, and so on. And within each nation's mission, each citizen has a special, personal mission.

It's clear to me that my unique mission is to teach Torah and Kabbalah. Of course, everyone has the obligation to teach the ways of God to their children (as it says in Deuteronomy 6:7). But my whole life involves performing the mission of teaching Torah; it permeates all my other obligations, such as honoring my parents, giving to charity, and visiting the sick. I know other people whose special mission is charity work—their whole being speaks charity. And there are some people whose mission is to teach others to be sensitive to how words can hurt or heal—how to speak kindly and not badly about others.

Sometimes people know their mission, and sometimes they don't know their mission. But that doesn't mean they're not performing it.

There's a beautiful story in the Talmud about Rabbi Tarfon, who was known to be an unusually loving and caring son.

One day Rabbi Tarfon became terminally ill. His mother went to the sages and asked them to please pray for her son. "He is such a wonderful son," she told them. "I don't know if there's any son in the world who honors his mother as much as my son honors me. He honors me more than enough."

The sages responded, "Your son honors you more than enough? If your son honored you a thousand times more, it wouldn't come close to what he really should do for you."

Rabbi Tarfon's mother was shocked and disturbed by the sages' harsh words against her son. She was trying to build up a case for her son's recovery by praising his great deeds, and the sages are telling her these deeds were far from sufficient.

Why did the sages do this? They were concerned that this mother was actually undermining her son's recovery by singing his praises. By saying, "My son has honored me more than enough," she may be saying, although unintentionally, that her son's mission was finished in this world and he doesn't need to be here any longer.

His mother mistakenly assumed that his mission was to be a great teacher. However, the sages knew better. They realized that Rabbi Tarfon's mission on earth may very well have been to grow in honoring his mother. And if that were the case, then all his mother's praises for her loving son were actually preventing his recovery. Because if he had honored her more than enough, then he had completed his mission on earth and was no longer needed.

When you complete your mission, you're out of here.

The sages, therefore, started to argue with her, insisting that he hadn't even come close to fulfilling his mission in this world.

Of course, even people who think they know their mission might be mistaken. For example, I say that my mission is to teach Torah and Kabbalah, but perhaps it's to be an attentive father, who needs to succeed at balancing his private life and his public life. For example, even if I became a successful teacher and best-selling author, I could be failing at my mission if I neglected my family in the process. In working so hard to become a worldwide influential teacher, am I really concerned about serving God, or is it all a cleverly camouflaged ego trip?

I know a man who invests all of his energy in helping the homeless. He has been honored by the mayor and many organizations in his city for the shelters he has built and programs he has initiated. But he hasn't visited his father, who is in a nursing home, for many months, so preoccupied is he with fulfilling his mission. It is no coincidence that helping the homeless brings him a lot of satisfaction and that he doesn't get along so well with his father. He has convinced himself that shortchanging his obligation to honor his father is legitimate in the name of his higher service to God.

But the mission is never so simple or so self-gratifying. More often than not, whatever it is that stretches you as a human being may be the very thing you've been placed on earth to confront and resolve.

Often, your mission is purposely obscure. If it was so obvious, we would be prone to put aside everything else but that. However, there are many obligations we are required to fulfill even if they don't relate directly to our personal mission, because they relate to our overall mission as human beings, as members of our communities and nations.

All in all, it is important to remember that even if you are not sure what your precise personal mission is—even if you don't feel as if you're fulfilling your mission—you may in fact be on target. This is one of the most important lessons of the Torah and Kabbalah. Each and every one of us has a divine purpose and mission on earth.

How to Find Your Mission

By now I am sure you are wondering how you can find out what is your calling and mission. The Vilna Gaon, who was one of the greatest Jewish sages of the eighteenth century, tells us how.

He quotes Proverbs (3:6)—"In all your ways know God and He will straighten your path"—and explains the difference between a "way" and a "path": A "way" is known to everyone. It's the highway. Everyone knows where the highway is. It's a public thoroughfare. But a "path" is off the beaten track. A path is not public. It is the private and unique way for the individual.

There are certain ways that we serve God that are common to us all. These ways are not unique to any of us. They are the highways of life. You can't get anywhere unless you get on those highways. However, once you get on the public highway, suddenly you will see a sign that says, "David—exit 3 miles left." That is where David turns off to continue his journey to fulfill his mission. Now, Jan, who was also on the highway, sees David get off and feels a little jealous. "Lucky guy! He found his path." But with some patience Jan plods forward until she discovers her path. And sure enough, there's a sign for her too. "Jan—5 miles exit left."

Everyone has a unique path waiting for them to journey upon. To find it we've got to get on the highway. Collectively we have a mission. It's the highway. The collective mission of human beings is to become more and more humane.

Each nation has a mission. One nation may be responsible to lead the advancement of technology in the world. Another perhaps is meant to lead research and development in the field of medicine. Another perhaps is called upon to increase art and music. And yet another may be appointed to head up promoting the moral and ethical progress of the world.

After we have accepted our mission as a member of the human race and our mission as a member of our specific nation, then we will be we shown our individual mission. Until that time you should work at becoming a more decent human being and a better citizen of your nation. When you are on the public highway, God will lead to your unique path.

Walking with God

In the world of business, if your company sends you on a mission, the boss generally stays at the office while you go off to accomplish the assigned task. But that's not the case when God sends you on a mission. God comes along.

This is the meaning of the verse in Psalms 127: "If God doesn't build your house, your labor is for nothing."

Now, you might think that if God is going to build your house, why should you have to labor at all? The Psalm is saying that you must labor nonetheless, but if you don't invite God into your work, your efforts will be worthless. You will not have the energy to achieve your task. You can choose to build a house, you can haul the bricks and the mortar, but, without God, Who is the power source, your house will never get built in a meaningful way.

This is what's unusual about our mission from God. The One who sends us joins us in our mission. But if we don't acknowledge His presence in our work, then we are powerless to truly succeed.

The daily focus of our life should be all about inviting God to join us in the performance of our mission.

A famous story tells about a man who dreamed that he saw his whole life's journey as footsteps in the sand. Sometimes there were two imprints—his and God's. But during the parts of the trek that were most difficult, he saw only one set of footprints. He complained to God, "God, You promised me that You would always accompany me in my journey. How is it that during the most difficult times in my life, You disappeared?" God responded, "I have always been with you. The reason why you only see one set of footprints is because during your most difficult times, I carried you. Those footprints are Mine."

It is especially helpful to remember this in the most challenging moments.

During times of pain in your life have you ever asked, "Why is God doing this to me? Why is God hurting me?"

There is no answer to that question because it is the wrong question. This question is based on a perception that God is an invisible Being floating somewhere in outer space, while you are down here on earth, separate and removed from Him. However, Kabbalah says that there is no such God and there is no such you. The true you is the soul, and the soul is none other than a spark of God.

Therefore, the real question is, "Why is God doing this to an aspect of Himself?"

I admit that this question also has no answer; however, I think there is great comfort in knowing that you are not alone in your pain, that God is never out to get you, that whatever you are going through, God completely shares. Remember, whatever God puts you through is also what He puts Himself through, because you are a soul, an expression of God.

If you embrace this consciousness, then you will draw upon divine strength and find great courage. You will rise to the occasion, overcome the challenge confronting you, and experience the triumph of the spirit.

BEATING JEALOUSY

Once you understand that life is a divine mission, you will realize that no one has a better or more important mission than you. It is ridiculous to ever be envious of another person's lot. Don't ever think that the president of the United States is any more important than a waiter in a restaurant. If God is with us in our mission, then one person's mission cannot be more important than another's, because everyone's mission is actually God's mission.

Real success does not depend on how much we accomplish on earth. And it does not have anything to do with how much attention the accomplishment gains in the public eye. What really matters is your intention and the quality of your deeds. Did you put your soul into your mission and live your life for God's sake, seeking to grow, striving to become better, concerned about improving yourself and the world?

The great Torah sages taught: I am a creation and my friend (even one who is uneducated) is a creation. Just as he is not an expert in what I do, I am not an expert in what he does. Do not think that I do more and he does less. That is incorrect. It does not matter whether he accomplishes seemingly big deeds or little ones. What really matters is whether his intentions are for the sake of heaven.

This lesson does not make any apparent sense. These great sages made historic contributions to human spiritual and ethical development. Their names will be remembered forever. How could they have possibly compared themselves to simple people who were unlearned, whose deeds could never have earned them world recognition, and who will surely be forgotten in the annals of history? How could they say that what really matters is the purity of one's intentions and the power of one's commitment to act on behalf of God?

These sages understood that each and every one of us has a mission in life—a calling. The thing you must always remember is *who* is calling. God is calling you to be His agent on earth, and the mission He is asking you to fulfill is not only your mission but God's mission.

If we are all working for God, then there is no such thing as a small mission. How could one divine mission be less than another divine mission? Can either one ever be any less than the ultimate?

If we would internalize this truth, we would free ourselves of the foolish habit of comparing ourselves with others. We would heal ourselves of a debilitating disease that rots our bones—jealousy.

The Talmud tells a story about a fellow who got a glimpse of the afterlife. He was surprised to see that the next world was upside down. He saw some people who during their lives on earth were very respected and famous, but in the next world they were nobody. Although these people were once recognized as significant members of the upper echelons of society, they were now considered part of the lower class. He also saw people who in their lifetimes were simple workers but now were prominent members of the highest order.

It was a shock to him.

Imagine you are a world-renowned actor and wherever you

go people look at you in great awe and admiration. Then the curtain falls on your life, and you find yourself in a new world—the afterlife. To your surprise, in this world nobody even notices you. Suddenly you see a familiar face, and it is your maid surrounded by a crowd of angelic fans. In the afterlife she may be the celebrity and you the shlepper. How is this possible? It all depends on the quality of your deeds and your attitude. Did you invite God into your work? Did you work with the intention of being God's agent, or was it just an ego trip?

In Summary

The commandments of the Torah are not just a bunch of good deeds to do. They are not simply instructions for living. They are much more than that. They articulate a lofty divine mission. It is such an exalted mission that even the angels wanted it when it was first offered. They could not understand why a frail human being, so prone to mistakes, so filled with negative and destructive urges, would be given such a mission. But the mission wasn't given to angels.

In fact, the mission was given to human beings precisely because we are not perfect angels. Our qualification for receiving it is that we are human beings who make mistakes and struggle to improve ourselves. In fact, our chief qualification for this great mission is our potential to fail and our potential to do evil. This is our greatness. Our problems are exactly the raw material for our elevation. This is because our mission is to grow. Our mission is to reveal a dynamic perfection of becoming. Our mission is to overcome our failings, choose goodness, and grow on behalf of God.

Our mission in life is our meaning in life. Unfortunate is the person who thinks he or she doesn't have a mission in life. Nietzsche, the German philosopher famous for saying that God is dead, ironically insisted that "unless a person feels that some infinite whole is working through him, his life has no meaning."

That "infinite whole" is God, and every one of His commandments is an opportunity to experience that profound meaning. Every one of His commandments empowers us to fix ourselves, our community, and this world for God's sake.

Our divine mission is the ultimate gift from the Ultimate One.

3

Absolutely You

DOES GOD NEED YOU?

A lot and not at all.

As we discussed earlier, when God chose (so to speak) to express the *possibility* of His becoming perfect, the creation of humanity became a necessary vehicle for the expression of this aspect of Divinity. However, the reason I emphasize the "possibility" is to remind us that God doesn't *have to* express becoming perfect but is *free* to do so. God did not have to create us; He chose to create us.

And it is precisely this idea that is the foundation of our great human dilemma, our existential crisis, our insistence on our significance and yet our struggle with our disposability. In seconds we can flip-flop from feeling confident in our role, needed at our jobs, essential to our families, to feeling insecure, dispensable, and replaceable. We feel at once very necessary and yet unnecessary.

At times we are poignantly aware of this; at other times, it haunts us subconsciously. But whenever we try to discern the meaning and value of our existence, this hidden angst is at the heart of it. We are constantly asking what is the significance and meaning of our existence.

To better understand our dilemma and to ultimately transcend it, we must start off where we always start off—with God. That's where everything starts.

According to Kabbalah, God is the absolute reality—the One who was, is, and always will be. That ultimate reality must be. In philosophical terminology, God is referred to as "the necessary existence" or "the necessary reality." If anything's going to be, then God must be. There must be an absolute, original, timeless reality that was, is, and always will be.

That's what we mean when we use the Tetragrammaton, the never-pronounced name of God consisting of four Hebrew letters, YHVH—an amalgam of the verb "to be" in the past, present, and future—was/is/and/will be.

At age six my son Yehuda repeatedly asked me who created God. And I repeatedly tried to explain to him that that nobody created God, because if "somebody" created "God," that somebody would *be* God. And that God always was, is, and will be. But as hard as I tried, he always said, "Oh, come on, Daddy, who created God?" Of course, in the mind of a child who is not yet ready for abstract ideas, God is pictured as an invisible being floating in space. And just as everyone else in space came from somewhere, God must have come from somewhere.

For the mature mind, however, it's critical to understand that when we speak about God, we are actually referring to the original reality who was, is, and always will be. God was not created. God simply was, is, and will always be. (For more on this see chapter 1 of my book *Seeing God*.)

And therefore, in a manner of speaking, we would say that although God has to be, God does not have to create you and me. We do not have to be.

God, the Ultimate Reality, necessarily exists, but the world does not necessarily exist.

This is a basic principle in Kabbalah. God created the world. And why did God create the world? For no reason. God didn't have to create the world. God has to be, but God doesn't have to become. And that means that God did not have to create us—He creates by absolute free choice.

What is free about absolute free choice?

God wanted to create, so He created. God wanted to express a process of becoming, so He created this imperfect world and an imperfect character—the human being—who strives and works to become more perfect.

Absolute free choice has no reason. If it had a reason, then it would be the reason that is motivating and compelling it, and it would no longer be free choice. If there's a reason to create, then the creative act isn't free, but rather it is the necessary outcome of that reason. Therefore, when Kabbalah talks about why God created the world, it is not asking "For what reason?" but rather, "For what *purpose?*"

To illustrate this point, if I ask you, "Why did Bell invent the telephone?" I could be asking you one of two implied questions: (1) "For what reason did he invent the telephone?" or (2) "For what purpose did he invent the telephone?" Now, nobody knows the reason why Bell invented the telephone. It could have been because his mother was on his case, saying, "Alex, get a job! You're a nobody. Be somebody!" Or because he was courting a pretty damsel and wanted to impress her with his ingenuity. We don't know the reason. We do, however, know the purpose for which he invented the telephone. He invented the telephone as a means of speaking to someone at a distance. That's what it's *for*—communication.

When we talk about God, we are not simply saying we don't know the reason why God created the world, but rather that *there really is no reason.* There's a purpose for which God created the world, but not a reason. Although the world is purposeful, it is still unreasonable.

It can be a bit disturbing to realize that your existence is basically unreasonable, that your existence is basically unnecessary. There is no compelling reason for your existence. Your existence is based on nothing other than the pure free will of God. God didn't have to create you, had no reason to create you; He simply wanted to. When you look at the world from this perspective, the world essentially feels absurd—this vast universe and everyone within it can exist as easily as not. It could be here one moment and gone the next.

The distinction between God and us is that God's existence is absolute and necessary, but human existence is not absolute and not necessary. Human existence is mere possibility—God didn't have to express the possibility of His becoming perfect, but when He did express it, the creation of humanity became a necessary vehicle for this aspect of Divinity.

However, God did not have to express this type of perfection. And, although He did and humanity became necessary, that still doesn't mean that the individual you and I must be. Nor does it mean that this type of perfection must continue to exist. God at any moment could choose to no longer express dynamic perfection.

Admittedly, this doesn't make us feel so good. Of course, we can say there's a purpose to the world, but hearing that our existence is unreasonable and unnecessary—that we can exist as easily as not—makes us feel rather disposable, like so many paper plates discarded when the picnic is over. Therefore, one of the basic drives of human beings is to justify our existence and make ourselves feel needed. We want to be absolute and necessary like God. Remember, before the vessels broke they got a taste of the Endless Light of God—the light of absolute necessary reality. Therefore, we who are those broken vessels are born in this world yearning to reclaim that feeling of necessary existence.

We human beings spend an inordinate amount of time and energy justifying our existence. Ultimately, however, we are like the employee who works hard and strives to be indispensable, bragging, "Without me, this business would fall apart. I have to be."

But who says the *business* has to be in the first place? Indeed, the business is totally dispensable. So we end up feeling like a dog that is chasing its tail in trying to find another reason for our existence.

GOD THE ABSOLUTE

One of the basic teachings of Torah and Kabbalah is that we do not have an independent existence. It's true that our bodies seem to suggest that we do have an independent existence. There's something about the physical body that suggests, "I'm my own person. I'm independent. I don't need anyone." But this is an illusion. We are not independent. We are not self-sufficient. We are not self-defined. No such thing!

At Isralight, I often invite the participants to take their pulse, close their eyes, and contemplate its significance. I ask: "Who decides that the beat goes on?"

We rarely appreciate how totally dependent we are. We totally depend upon God for every moment of our existence. God doesn't need us in order to exist Himself, but we need God. Right this second we exist only because God wants us to exist. If God didn't want us to exist at this moment, we would cease to be.

In other words, the foundation of our existence is mere possibility, completely dependent upon God. Therefore, no one else but God absolutely exists.

To understand this concept better, consider the following exercise. Stop reading right now and create a man (or woman) in your mind. Now, where does that person exist? Within your mind. Does that person have independent existence? No. He exists only as long as you continue to think about him. At the moment you stop thinking about him and resume reading, he no longer exists. Now, imagine this exercise from the perspective of the man in your mind. Let's say the man in your mind had consciousness. From his perspective, he would think, "There's me and there's my creator." But the truth is, there's really only his creator. He exists only within his creator; he doesn't have an independent existence. He is a mere possibility in your mind; he exists only by your desiring him into existence. And at the moment when you start to think, "What do I want to eat for dinner?" this man ceases to exist. Therefore, you can't say, "There's me and there is this man." There's really just you, yet in a mysterious way there is this man in your mind. And although this man is not you, although he is other than you, and although he doesn't have to exist, he is an expression of you.

And this is also true about our relationship to God. Although we are other than God, and although we do not have to exist, we are an expression of God, who must exist. In other words, we are unnecessary manifestations of the necessary. Therefore, although something about us feels disposable, yet there is also a feeling that we are absolute and necessary. And here lies the root of our dilemma.

Of course, the Thinker-Thought metaphor only explains part of the nature of existence. The man in your mind does not have free choice, while we, in relation to God, do. (We will take up this issue in the next chapter.)

WHO, ME? INSECURE?

I've been involved in education for more than fifteen years, and I used to think that some people are secure and some people are insecure. But as I came to know my students on a deeper level, I discovered that none of them were truly secure. By definition, if you're human, you're insecure, because your existence doesn't have to be. You don't have to exist, and yet you feel in some way that you do, because you are a soul, a spark of the absolute God.

When you realize that there's no reason for you to exist, you feel a certain absurdity in your own existence, and yet you sense that this can't be right. So you try to justify your existence. But can you think of anything you could do that would make you necessary? You have to admit that life could go on without you. That's the frightening implication of death. Death continually tells you, "You don't have to be." Worse than death is this insidious insecurity that death fosters—the fear of death. The actual experience of death occurs only once to each of us. And for many of us, who may die in our sleep or suddenly of a heart attack, the experience of death will not even be painful. The fear of death, however, occurs every single day, whether consciously or unconsciously; it is a chronic pain.

A story is told about a deal between two rabbis. They agreed that whichever one of them died first would come back in a dream and tell the survivor what the transition into the next world was like. In due time, one of them died. The other one waited, and sure enough, his friend came to him in a dream and said, "Hey, here I am. Now I'm on the other side."

"Wow, how was it?"

"Awesome. The Angel of Death pulled me out of my body like a hair being pulled out of cream."

"It was that easy? Unbelievable!"

"But I tell you right now, if they force me to come back, I will put up the biggest fight."

"Why? Now you know the secret of death."

"It's not death that bothers me. It's the fear of death. If I come back into the world, I'll forget, and again I'll be afraid of death."

Why are we afraid of death? Because death reminds us that we are a mere possibility. We could be here today and gone tomorrow. Even someone who is successful and important and having a major impact on the world could die suddenly without warning. That's why all Americans over age forty remember exactly where they were when they heard that John F. Kennedy had been assassinated. JFK was the most important person in the United States. Not only was he the president of the world's most powerful country, but in the eyes of many Americans, he was in the midst of leading the country into a new era of idealism. He was indispensable. Then, one Friday morning, sometime between breakfast and sixth-period geography, JFK was no more. A catastrophic reminder that we just simply don't have to be.

The whole Book of Ecclesiastes reiterates this idea of the existential condition of humanity being transient, unnecessary, and unreasonable: "Futility of futilities, all is futility." Life, the world, ourselves, all of it is nothing; it's a vapor. It looks substantive, but it doesn't have real substance. It's disposable.

People often try to overcome their existential insecurity by owning property, buildings, and other forms of material wealth commonly known as securities.

Once a couple invited me to teach their friends about Kabbalah, and thus generate funds for Isralight. It was an elegant occasion. The setting was their mansion, the caterer was the last word in gourmet, and the waiters and waitresses wore white gloves. "Unbelievable!" I thought, "This is going to be a big success."

When I started giving my class, Harry, my host, was sitting right in front of me. Within two minutes he got up and left. I was crushed. I thought, "Oh, my gosh, what did I do wrong? Did I say something offensive? In just two minutes, I turned my host off."

About five minutes later, Harry came back. He sat down at the back of the room. A few minutes later, he got up again and walked out. When he came back, he stood at the door. He did this so many times, I was getting upset. I didn't know what was going on.

After the class, I was sitting around with some of the guests and my hosts. One of the host's friend said, "Harry, it's great that you built a new swimming pool. How much did it cost you?"

He said, "You know, I was thinking about it. I projected that if I swim in the swimming pool every day for ten years, based on the amount of strokes that I would actually do, each stroke would have cost me fifty cents."

The other people laughed, but Harry was obviously serious.

As we were leaving, it started to rain, really pour. We pulled out of the driveway, and I saw Harry, my multimillionaire host, walk out of his house and head down the street in the pouring rain, without an umbrella, without a coat. His friend turned to me and said, "Poor man!"

"Poor man?" I asked in surprise.

"Yes, poor man!" the friend continued. "Couldn't you see how he couldn't even sit in your class for a moment? He's always like that. He cannot sit. People say he doesn't even sleep. He's always walking the streets at night."

Ethics of the Fathers (*Pirkei Avot*), a collection of wisdom from the sages that is included in the Talmud, proclaims: "The more you have, the more you worry." You worry that you're going to lose what have. You know that having these things is only in the realm of pure possibility and it could be as easily gone as it is easily here. That's the insecurity.

MADE OF FREE WILL

Philosophers and scientists since ancient times have tried to figure out of what elements human beings are made. Kabbalah says we're made of free will. We are a free expression of God's free will. Our existence is only mere possibility. And this adds more fuel to the fire of our insecurity burning away at our feelings of significance. The substance of life is free will. But what is free will? Free will is pure possibility. And that's what we are.

Our essence is freedom. On the one hand, we strive to be who we are. And who are we? We are pure possibility, pure freedom. Therefore, we can't help wanting to be free and do what we feel. Freedom gives us great pleasure. On the other hand, freedom gives us great pain.

Erich Fromm's classic *Escape from Freedom* elaborates on this idea that human beings also experience freedom as painful.

We human beings live within a paradox. We want to be free, and we don't want to be free. We have a love-hate relationship with our freedom. We hate being free, because it reminds us that we are pure possibility, we're not necessary. Nothing we do has to be. We could do this or we could do that. We could do that or we could do this. And that's really frightening. What ultimate difference does my choice make? If freedom of choice means I can do what I please, then it means that what I do is arbitrary. It means what I do isn't necessary, because if it was necessary, then why would I have the freedom to choose? I would *have* to do it. But I don't have to do anything, because I'm free. This is why we hate freedom, because freedom reminds us of our insecurity.

People really want to be imprisoned. They don't necessarily want to be in a penitentiary, but they feel comfortable and safe in their own prison. They want to be able to say, "I had no choice. This is what had to happen." It feels good. That's why people go to psychics, to palm readers, to Tarot card readers. They want to be relieved of the burden of an uncertain future. "Tell me what has to be, so now I don't have to choose it." Freedom gives us pleasure, and freedom gives us pain. It expresses who we are—manifestations of God's free will. But it also reminds us of who we are—mere possibility.

Escaping the Dilemma

Throughout the ages, human beings have devised ways to overcome their existential insecurity with being mere possibility and to relieve themselves of the pain of freedom of choice.

Solution number one: Deny!

Denial is a fantastic way to deal with problems. I deny that I'm pure possibility. I'm not pure possibility. Who said I'm pure possibility? Who says the world is created at all? Who said God created the world out of free choice and the world didn't have to be? The world had to be. Nature is a necessary outcome, an expression of the absolute reality. Nature is merely a different mode of eternity.

This was Baruch Spinoza's position. The controversial seventeenth-century theologian argued that nature is God. Nature is absolute. It wasn't created. It always was. It is. It will be. It is necessary. Man, as part of nature, is necessary. We're not possibility, not unreasonable. We are a different mode of absolute reality. Therefore, freedom is an illusion. Everything is predetermined, in the same way that an oak seed produces an oak tree, and the oak tree produces oak seeds.

This view, known as pantheism, is essentially idolatry. What was the position of the idolater? Nature has to be. Nature is absolute, necessary reality. By merging with nature, humans achieve security.

Ancient man was insecure, so he found security by merging with nature. If you ever wander around the ancient history wing of a museum, you may be surprised to see that many of the idols of pagan civilizations were animals. They idolized animals. Why would a human being idolize an animal? Because they believed that animals were on a higher level than human beings. These ancient peoples aspired to be like animals, because an animal is purely natural, driven by instinct, uncomplicated by the crazy idea of free choice.

Modern paganism also idolizes nature. That's why the goal is to "flow with nature," to do what comes naturally. Of course, what comes naturally might be to leave your wife and kids to have fun with a sprite who is twenty years your junior. All kinds of heinous acts are perpetrated by seemingly good people who say, "It just came to me." The assumption is that if it is natural, it is good. This is idolatry.

This is why the Torah is so adamantly against idolatry. If you've ever read the Torah, you may wonder why it comes down so heavily on idolaters. I mean, what do you care if somebody feels like bowing down to a rock or a tree? It's a free world. If somebody wants to bow down to a rock or a tree, why should it bother me? Idolatry, however, isn't just about people bowing down to trees. It is deifying nature. Idolatry is a worldview where anything that is natural is good.

The worst outbreak of modern-day paganism was Nazism. Essentially, Adolf Hitler was a pagan. Here's what Hitler said in

Mein Kampf: "In nature, there is no pity for the lesser creatures when they are destroyed, so that the fittest may survive. Going against nature brings ruin to man. It is only Jewish impudence to demand that we overcome nature."

Basically, he was saying, when a lion devours a zebra, is that wrong? Isn't that what must be? Isn't that nature? The survival of the fittest is nature. We human beings shouldn't squelch our nature. It's only the Jews and their Torah who insist that you can overcome nature. Indeed, the Torah teaches that you must rise above nature by elevating everything natural rather than succumbing to it.

Again, to quote from Hitler: "It is true we are barbarians. That is an honorable title to us. . . . I free humanity from the shackles of the soul, from the degrading suffering caused by the false vision called conscience and ethics. The Jews have inflicted two wounds on mankind: circumcision on its body and conscience on its soul. They are Jewish inventions. The war for domination of the world is waged only between these two of us, between these two camps, the Germans and the Jews. Everything else is but deception." Hitler was a true pagan, and he recognized that the set of beliefs that the Jews had brought to the world were antithetical to paganism.

Ritual circumcision, which brings a male baby into the covenant of Abraham, makes a statement that nature can be improved upon by human spiritual aspirations. Conscience, the other "scourge" that Hitler correctly attributed to the Jews, obligates adherence to moral laws above "doing what comes naturally."

Paganism, by making nature absolute, is one solution to human existential insecurity. Another, opposite solution is to simply accept your existence as unnecessary, as absurd, as nothing. Strive to become nothing, which you essentially are.

Philosophies such as that advocated by Arthur Schopenhauer in the nineteenth century are based on this conclusion. So are some Eastern religions that strive to achieve *nirvana,* which is "nothingness," or "extinction" (of the individual ego in the

Absolute). All desires must be quelled, for desires inevitably lead to suffering. Some of these religions eschew all absolutes, including any concept of God; a human being fulfills his or her highest potential by entering a state of nothingness.

Between believing that you are absolute or believing you are nothing, there is another way to solving the problem—the way of commandments.

SOLVING INSECURITY

King Solomon in his Book of Ecclesiastes grapples with the devastating awareness that our existence is seemingly absurd:

> *Utter futility! . . . Utter futility! All is futile! What real value is there for a person in all his work under the sun?* (1:2–3)

In other words, there's no substance to our life; we don't have to be. But after describing a long journey of trial and error, anticipation and disappointment, after much painstaking personal spiritual turmoil, King Solomon surprises us with a short and poignant ultimate answer:

> *In the end, after all is said and done, revere God, live by His commandments—for this is the all of man.* (12:13)

How does fulfilling God's commandments solve our existential crisis of insecurity? How do commandments solve our conflict between the desire for freedom and the desire to feel that who we are and what we do is necessary?

The oft-repeated complaint about commandments is that they take away freedom. If we are commanded "You shall not steal," for example, then our freedom to steal is gone.

Moses, in the Book of Deuteronomy (30:19), delineates the archetypal choice situation:

*"I [God] have set before you today the blessing and
the curse, life and death. Choose life. . . ."*

But wait a second! What kind of choice do I have if someone
tells me what to choose? It's like saying, "Here, I'm giving you
a choice between a Chevrolet and a Ford. Choose Chevrolet . . .
or suffer the consequences."

You still have the freedom to choose, because, even knowing
the consequences, you can still choose Ford. And when you
think about it, if your choices incurred no consequences, then
there would be no meaning to your choice. What difference will
it make if you choose to do an act or not do it if there are no
consequences?

If you want to express your true self as a free being, and yet
also feel that you are absolute and necessary, you will freely
choose precisely that which you are commanded to do, that
which you *must* do. And that brings resolve to the problem of
your existential insecurity.

Being told what to choose is not the problem. In fact, it's the
solution. The solution is for us to *freely choose* to take up our
divine mission and be a vehicle for God, who is absolute and
necessary.

In other words, commandments empower human beings to
bond with the absolute, and the absolute is God. I overcome the
insecurity of being unnecessary and fulfill my desire for freedom
by *choosing* to do a mission for the One who is necessary. And
when you do that, you experience the truth about yourself,
which you intuited all along—you are a spark of the absolute
God. And you will never die. You may leave your body and this
world, but you will exist eternally at one with God.

How do I (a being who is only pure possibility) bond with
God, the absolute reality? Through the commandments, which
contain the expressed will of God. I choose to do what I have to
do and to do it for the One who has to be. I freely accept my
mission to be God's agent.

Unless a spiritual path can articulate for me the expressed

will of God—telling me exactly what God requires of me, what I must do for God—there is no way I can ever bridge the gap between my futile human existence and God's absolute reality. I can never overcome my existential conflict between feeling like nothing and yet yearning for absolute existence.

Kabbalah teaches that a human being finds peace only in God. He will find no rest anywhere else. If we are restless and insecure, it is because we have not committed ourselves to working for God. The more human beings yearn to connect with God in their lives and make God part of their lives by serving Him, the more they experience absolute existence and inner peace.

The only way we can truly bond with God is by making His will our will, being His agent, and performing His mission. Nowadays, many people who want to come close to God practice various types of meditation toward that end.

I don't believe that because people *feel* they are coming close to God that they necessarily *are* coming close to God. In fact, very often the people who feel they are closest to God are the ones who are farthest away. They are living in total subjectivity. Their spiritual experiences are illusions.

Of course, it is possible to access the real thing through meditation. The only way to tell the real meditation from the illusory is to watch and see whether the person's meditation inspires them to align themselves with God's will by fulfilling His commandments and striving to grow, choose goodness, and improve themselves and the world.

A man can spend ten hours a day in meditation and claim to be close to God, but if he commits adultery, everyone realizes he's a phony.

Only the commandments, the expressed will of God—not meditation alone—enables the human being to bond with the Divine. The commandments are the bridge between the human being who is pure possibility and the Divine, who is the absolute reality. Through the commandments we experience ourselves as part of the Absolute; we discover that our true inner self is none other than an expression of the Absolute. We then feel filled with a profound sense of security and peace.

The path of commandment gives me the choice. I can choose what I must do, or I can choose not to do what I must do. I can work for God and experience myself as part of the Absolute, or I can work for myself, do as I please, and feel unnecessary and disposable. Of course that would be ridiculous. When God commands, "Choose life," and that means, "eternal life," can you imagine responding: "No! I want freedom, so I'll choose eternal death and suffer the insecurity and angst of being a mere possibility, and never discover my true inner self."

Although pure possibility can sometimes appear attractive, in reality it is torture. Imagine waking up every morning and having nothing that you have to do, nothing you're supposed to do. You can do as you please. So you wake up, and you don't have to brush your teeth, you don't have to get the kids off to school, you don't have to eat breakfast, go to aerobics class, answer your telephone messages, go shopping for something you need, visit a friend, or read the Sunday paper. The euphoric feeling of freedom that you might at first experience would, within a little while, be replaced by anxiety. That's why, even on vacations, we plan what to do. We have to get up and go to the beach, or take a hike, or tour Prague. Having *nothing* that we must do is paralyzing rather than freeing. But even with the best of plans, unless we have something we must do for God, then we will never overcome the suffering caused by our existential insecurity.

The solution to our existential insecurity is to make God's will our will and fulfill His commandments. This is how we can satisfy our paradoxical cravings. On the one hand, we crave to be free because free will is the very essence of our being. On the other hand, we crave to feel absolute and necessary. When we follow the path of the commandments, we get it all.

When we freely choose to do what we must do and dedicate ourselves to serving the One who must be, then we experience the truth about who we really are—sparks of the Absolute bonded with the Absolute.

Choosing to Be Commanded

At the very beginning of the Torah's account of Abraham's spiritual journey, we read:

> God said to Abram, "Go for yourself from your land . . . to the land that I will show you. . . . So Abram went as God had told him." (Genesis 12:1, 4)

The classical commentaries point out the difference between the Hebrew verb *said* and the Hebrew verb *told*, which has the connotation of a commandment. God did not command Abraham (then known as Abram) to go. Rather, God "said" that he should go, in the sense of offering advice. But Abraham understood something very profound. He understood that the greatest fulfillment of a human being is to *choose* to be commanded. Abraham wanted to be commanded, because he understood the secret that if there's nothing I *have* to do for God in this world, then I have no connection to the Absolute and my existence will be arbitrary.

Although God advised Abraham, "Go for yourself," Abraham wanted more. He did not want to go just for himself; he wanted to go for God. He wanted to turn this free journey into a divine mission, be God's agent, and become a vehicle for God.

God gives each one of us the same opportunity—to bond with the Absolute, the necessary—by giving us each a mission to accomplish on His behalf. And we can either choose to fulfill our mission or not.

The commandments offer us this opportunity. The irony, which we'll deal with in the next chapter, is essentially that, whatever I choose, I can't really avoid my mission.

But the question is: Do I choose it freely, thus overcoming my existential insecurity and experiencing my connection to the Absolute? Or do I end up doing it anyway without even knowing that I did it and living with a whole lot of angst in the meantime?

What has to be has to be. Our real choice is whether we choose to know it, feel it, and celebrate it.

In Summary

Our existential condition is insecurity. We have a love-and-hate relationship with our freedom. We love our freedom because it expresses who we are—free beings made of free will. However, our freedom reminds us that our existence is pure possibility; we do not have to exist, and if we are free to do as we please, then our lives add up to nothing.

What fills our free choices with a sense of eternal meaning or ultimate value? How can we take our futile existence and merge it with absolute reality?

The answer is by following the commandments—choosing to do what we must do and doing it for God. Choosing fulfills our need to express our free selves. But choosing to do what we must and doing it for God's sake, as God's agent, binds our free selves to God. This brings us ultimate meaning. This is the only formula that will ever bring peace to our existential dilemma.

Going back to our original question: How much does God need us? It depends on us—on the choices we make. The answer could be a lot or not at all. How absolute the quality of our existence is depends on us—whether we choose to do what we must do and be God's agent. Then we experience the godliness of our true inner self, the soul—a spark of the Absolute.

4

Your Ultimate Choice

IN THE MUSICAL *Fiddler on the Roof,* Tevye, the poor milkman who is fed up with eking out a meager living from his one poor cow, sings, "If I Were a Rich Man." He fantasizes how luxurious his life would be: a house with one long staircase going up, and one even longer coming down; his wife, Goldie, "with a proper double chin" . . . yelling at the servants; and seven hours a day to discuss the holy books. The song ends with a poignant question:

> Lord, who made the lion and the lamb,
> You decreed I should be what I am;
> Would it spoil some vast eternal plan,
> If I were a wealthy man?

Was Tevye destined to be poor, or could he have become rich in some way? What is the relationship between fate and free

choice? How free are we to determine the events and achievements of our lives? And to what extent does God really run the
world?

Free choice is the very basis of a life guided by the commandments. The essence of commandments is that you can
choose to obey them or disobey them and enjoy the rewards of
your choice or accept the consequences. If God didn't want us
to have free choice, He could have preprogrammed us to do His
will naturally and instinctively like animals. Animals do not
have commandments. Whatever an animal does is always
aligned with God's will. They do not have free choice, and they
are not liable for their actions.

The Oral Tradition states that the reason man was created
last in the story of creation was in order to teach us that if we
choose to do the will of God, then we are the pinnacle of creation. But if we choose to do other than God's will, then even a
tiny gnat precedes us in the line of creation and is closer to God,
the source of all.

In other words, when we choose to fulfill the commandments, we bond with God and thereby achieve the highest status
a created being could ever hope to achieve—godliness. But if we
don't, then a tiny gnat, who always does God's will, is closer to
the Absolute.

Free choice is necessary for us human beings to fulfill the
divine purpose for which we were created. Without free choice
there could be no commandments, no liability for our actions,
no struggle, no mission, and no meaning to life. If everything
were determined, if everything had been already plotted out by
God, then we would simply be puppets and the consequences
we enjoy or suffer from our actions would be arbitrary.

Maimonides, the great twelfth-century philosopher, explic-
itly delineated the significance of free choice:

> Permission is given to every human being. If one
> chooses to incline himself to a path of goodness and
> be righteous, the right is in his hands. If one chooses

to incline himself to a path of evil and be wicked, the right is in his hands. (*Mishna Torah, The Laws of Penitence*, 5)

In other words, you have a choice: you can be evil or you can be good. Maimonides continues:

> Don't be as the fools who say that being good or being evil is a decree from God. It is not so. Every individual is befitting to be good like Moses, our teacher, or an evil person like the evil king Jeroboam ben Navat [who split Israel into two kingdoms and built pagan shrines to golden calves].

So it seems as definite as black and white—there is free choice. You've got the choice to be good. You've got the choice to be evil. That seems to be the end of the story.

I wish it were the end of the story. It would have made this chapter much easier to write. This issue, however, is one of the most complex in Torah and Kabbalah. I learned early on that we all have free choice. Years into my study of Kabbalah, I discovered a book entitled *Leshem Shevo ve-Echlamah** by a great Jerusalem Kabbalist, Rabbi Shlomo Eliyashev (1841–1925). In his book he presents traditional Jewish sources that express a shocking amount of determinism, which would seem to suggest that we are not free at all. But that can't be. The resolution to this dilemma requires the exploration of some very challenging ideas, but in the end it will all be much clearer.

GOD'S PLAN

Most people have heard the famous line from the Book of Ecclesiastes: "To everything there is a season and a time to every purpose under the heavens." The Midrash (rabbinic literature

---

*The title means "Jacinth, Agate, and Amethyst" (Exodus 28:19), a reference to the Torah's description of gems in the high priest's breastplate.

that elucidates nuances in the Five Books of Moses) elaborates, "There was a time for man to enter the Garden of Eden and a time for him to leave." But what about free choice? What if Adam had chosen not to eat from the Tree of Knowledge? Wouldn't he and his descendants have remained in Eden forever? According to the Midrash, he *had* to leave. Does that mean that his leaving, and therefore his sinning, was predetermined?

The Midrash continues: "There was a time for Noah to enter the ark and there was a time for him to leave." Was the Flood predetermined? Wasn't it the consequence of human beings making bad choices, choosing to commit crimes against each other instead of living in peace? But the Midrash seems to indicate that the Flood was inevitable. And wasn't Noah saved because of his good behavior, which he freely chose? Or was it his fate to enter the Ark, regardless of his choices and actions?

Again, the Midrash: "There was a time for Abraham to receive the covenant. And there was a time for the commandments to be given." Wasn't the covenant Abraham's reward for discovering the one ineffable God behind all creation? What if Abraham had chosen instead to stay in his father's idol-making business? Didn't Abraham have free choice? And didn't the Jewish people receive the commandments because they chose to accept them and live by them?

Yet the Midrash seems to be saying that all these times and events were already set up from the very beginning.

Elsewhere, the Midrash goes even further to exasperate our problem: "Many were designated prior to their coming. Death was ordained to come into the world, and God did not bring it except through the snake, who was preordained for it."

This statement seems to contradict the classic choice described in the Book of Genesis. Adam and Eve had to decide whether to eat from the Tree of Knowledge, and thus bring death into the world, or to obey God's commandment to abstain from eating from that particular tree. This Midrash implies that it was a setup, that death was preordained to come into the world, regardless of Adam and Eve's choice.

The Midrash proves its point by quoting a verse in Genesis (2:17):

> *And God commanded Adam, saying, "You may certainly eat from every tree in the garden, but from the Tree of Knowledge of Good and Evil you shall not eat from it. For on the day that you will eat from it, you will surely die."*

God wasn't saying "*If* you eat from it" or "Maybe you will eat from it." God was saying, "On the day that you will eat from it," meaning, "You *will* eat from it. I know I told you not to, but I know you are going to. And you *will* die."

If that's not enough, Psalms 66 gives us this:

> *Come and see the works of God, awesome are His schemes toward human beings.*

The Midrash, in explaining this Psalm, says that God had already orchestrated how death should come into the world through the human being.

The Midrash continues to discuss other events that were preordained and, if one reads it all, one might mistakenly conclude that there is no freedom, there are no choices, the script has already been written, and we are simply playing our assigned parts.

What then is the point of getting up tomorrow morning if I'm only going to be playing out a script that is already written?

Such reflections on fate and destiny may seem metaphysical, but in all of our lives we experience events and encounters that, in retrospect, seem destined to have happened to us. Did you ever have a fight with somebody that you were very close with? You're so furious that you decide to get on a plane and fly to the North Pole. The farther away, the better. You're checking into a 5-star igloo, and sure enough, who's checking in beside you? Your friend, trying to get the farthest away from you. And then you hear in the background the theme music of *The Twilight Zone.*

Sometimes we look back at the most significant meetings or events in our lives, and we do not feel that they were matters of chance, or of any conscious decision on our part. Ask a really well-matched couple, one of those perfect pairs, how they met. She was working behind the Customer Service desk, and he came in to exchange a malfunctioning cordless phone. And if he had not bought that lemon? If he had picked up the next box in the display, would they ever have met? Impossible! Or what about the president of a company who, at his retirement dinner, reveals that forty-five years ago a stranger sitting next to him on a park bench happened to mention to him that this company was looking for new blood?

The *Seder Olam* ("The Order of the World"), a chronicle of human history composed in the second century CE, states:

> God showed the first man [Adam] all of history. God showed him every leader of every generation, every prophet, every official, every person's particular task, etc. . . . God showed him the number of their days, the total of their hours, and even the sum total of their footsteps.

According to this, Adam knew each and every one of us. The first man knew that David Aaron was going to be red-haired and was going to live in Jerusalem and have seven kids. He knew that David Aaron was going to start the Isralight Institute and that he was going to write this book. So I feel silly remembering all the agonizing soul searching I went through deciding what I was going to do with my life, deciding whether to found Isralight, deciding whether to direct my energies toward writing a third book. I wasted my time. I should have asked the first man. He could have told me.

You probably think that you chose to buy this book, or to borrow it from a friend. But the first man knew that you would read this book. You could have gone into Barnes and Noble looking for a computer manual or a trashy novel, and somehow you had to walk out with this book in your hand. You could have gone to your friend's place for dinner or to watch a video, and somehow you had to borrow this book. Your plans today may have included going out on a hike, on a date, or to a good movie, and instead you are sitting here reading *The Secret Life of God*. And the first man knew you would be.

So what's going on here?

GOD THE AUTHOR

A teacher of mine once said, "When you make a bad choice between two options, it may not be a matter of a bad choice but simply a problem of poor imagination. There was a third option that you didn't even imagine existed."

Classically the philosophers have struggled for centuries over the question of free will versus determinism. However, maybe we simply have poor imagination and there is a third option beyond the either/or.

Before we can explore this third option, I want to remind you of the disclaimer I made at the very beginning: that whenever we speak about God, we are necessarily speaking in metaphors. I am about to present to you a metaphor that I hope will give you a different feeling about the choices you are making and show you how much God is involved in your life.

But this metaphor is just that—a metaphor. Sometimes people take metaphors referring to God literally. The standard metaphor of the relationship between God and humanity is king and subject, or parent and child. There are other metaphors: of husband and wife, or even God as the child and the human being as the mother. The more metaphors, the better, so that we don't get stuck in one metaphor and begin to think that's the reality. Each metaphor gives us a peephole into the different kinds of relationship we have with God. What follows is a new peephole.

God is our author and we are God's characters.

An author's writing is an act of self-expression. Every character in his book has a piece of himself in it. That's why creative writing classes always tell you to write about what you know. Don't write about geisha girls in Japan unless you were one; a novel about a woman from suburban New Jersey may be less dramatic, but it will be better written, because an author must know and relate to her characters. Each character expresses a different aspect of that author. Each character is created in the image of the author.

The Torah, in the Book of Genesis, makes an outlandish assertion. It says that God created man in His image. What's that supposed to mean? God created man in His image in the same way that an author creates all his characters in his image. Each character in the story expresses a different aspect of the author. Even the interaction between the characters is in some way an unfolding of the truth of the author.

On the other hand, there are other characters that the author doesn't identify with. Every good story has an antagonist, a villain. Every good book has a problem character who creates all the tension. Why is that character there? Because the villain plays the essential role of bringing out the inner selves of all the other characters. That's an important role. The role of the evil people in the story is to help the good people in the story reveal their deepest selves. The villain creates the opportunity for other characters to rise to their challenges and demonstrate extraordinary courage, tremendous fortitude, and new commitment.

The Talmud refers to the evil forces in the universe as the yeast in the dough. Yeast consists of microscopic fungal organisms. Who wants to eat fungal organisms? But it's the yeast in bread dough that acts as a catalyst to make the dough rise. So, too, evil was created in the world to be a catalyst for the growth and personal enrichment of others. It, too, is serving the author within the context of the whole story.

The Zohar, the classic work of Kabbalah, metaphorically describes evil in the world as a prostitute who has been hired by the king to seduce his son, the prince. Of course the king does not want her to succeed. However, he wants to create an opportunity for the prince to realize his own royal integrity by resisting this great temptation and choosing to act in the way that is befitting his nobility. Until this test, the son's royal status was merely an inherited title and a wardrobe of regal clothing but not the genuine expression of himself, accomplished through the power of his own choices and determined efforts.

The antagonist in every story is actually providing the opportunities for the other characters to make great choices that embody great goodness. The villain is actually serving the best interest of all the other characters, and, of course, the author (whom the story is really all about).

Therefore, every character is serving the author. However, some characters are serving the author directly, as direct expressions of himself in the world he created. And some are serving the author indirectly by creating opportunities for others to be of direct service.

This is the essence of all choices of every character. To serve or not to serve is not the question, and it is not the choice. Every character serves the author. The choice is only about how you serve—directly, playing the hero or heroine, or indirectly, playing the villain.

And what difference does it make if you serve directly or indirectly? It really does not make a difference to the author—his story will be written. But it sure does make a difference to you, the character. Your choices determine not only the outcome of your final scene but also the quality of your life throughout the whole story.

As we all know, the good guys win in the end. Sure, they might lose some battles along the way, but they always win the war. However, even when they appear to be losing, often they are really winning, because in every moment of their struggle they achieve personal transformation and enjoy a profound sense of identification with the author.

The Talmud teaches that the Shekhinah, the Divine Presence, which is the feminine manifestation of God (a subject we will take up in the next chapter), desires to live in this world. How? Through you and me when we choose to follow the commandments and directly serve God, the Author.

This is not the case for the villain. He is not only heading for the worst ending but even his journey, the quality of his daily living, is devoid of the divine fulfillment that life in this imperfect world offers.

The villain gets clobbered in the end. He may think he is a winner, but all his apparent successes are only setting him up for his ultimate demise. Worse than the great punishment that awaits him in the final scene is the pain he suffers daily over his existential insecurity. He is not striving to grow, overcome evil, and choose goodness. He is not interested in using his imperfections as a starting point toward becoming more perfect and thereby serving God and being His agent.

Therefore, the villain denies himself the greatest pleasure of all—living a life filled with God's Presence. His soul is alienated from its Divine Source, and his inner world has no connection with God's absolute reality and is therefore devoid of any lasting value or meaning.

In the world at large he may have much money, live in an elegant mansion, wear the most expensive and latest fashions, and act out all his sexual fantasies. But his inner world is hell. Indeed, he creates his own hell. "The evil ones are like the driven sea that cannot rest, and its waters throw up mire and mud. There is no peace, says God to the wicked" (Isaiah 57: 20–21).

Now we have a better understanding of the true meaning of "serving God" and "not serving God." Often, when people pick up the Bible and read about serving God, they feel put off, feeling: Why would I want to *serve* God? Be *servile*? It seems kind of demeaning. But if you're a character in the story, how could you not want to serve the author? It's who you are. And it's the greatest honor in the world.

What does it mean to serve the author directly?

It means that I am a vehicle for the expression of the author in this story. I can't wait to serve the author, because the more I serve the author, the more the author's presence permeates my very being, and the more I discover that I am actually a spark of the author. It's not about obedience. It's about self-expression. It's about who you are, why you are, who God is, and why He creates.

Kurt Vonnegut in *Breakfast of Champions* writes about an author who decides to enter into his story and introduce himself to his chief character. But the character runs away, refusing to accept that he has an author at all and that he is merely a figment of the author's imagination.

In stark contrast to Vonnegut's story, the Book of Genesis tells of an encounter between the Divine Author and one of His chief characters, Abraham. But the outcome is quite different. God, the Author, tells Abraham, "Are you willing to work with Me? Are you willing to serve Me? Are you willing to be the vehicle for My presence in this world? Because I want to participate in this world. And I want to live in it through you."

And Abraham answers with a resounding "Yes."

That's the story of the covenant of Abraham.

Using this metaphor of author-character, you can start looking at your life a little differently. You can say to yourself, "I really want to serve a higher purpose. I really want to fit into the greater story. I really want to directly serve God, the Author, and play my part the best way possible."

MONOLOGUE OR DIALOGUE?

Now let's address the question of whether we have free choice or whether our life is predetermined.

Is the story of life a monologue in which the author is talking in many different voices to himself through his characters and their lives are totally determined? Or is the story of life a dialogue, where the characters interact with the author and contribute to the story through their free choices?

The answer is yes and yes.

Free choice and determinism both exist simultaneously—the story of life is beyond either/or.

During the creative process, most great writers testify that, in their most luminous passages, their writing took on a life of its own. The characters came alive and contributed to the story.

And this is the mystery of history. It is both a monologue, so to speak, *within* God, scripted down to every detail, and yet it is paradoxically also a dialogue *between* God and us, His characters—a drama cowritten by God and man.

Ingmar Bergman, the famous director, was once asked, "How do you direct a film?" He answered:

> I don't direct films. I let films direct me. The most important thing in the creative job is to let your intuition tell you what to do. I am writing a script and the plan for this man is that he will do such and such; all these other things in the plot will then fall into place. But my intuition tells me suddenly that this man says he will not do such and such. So I ask my intuition why. And the intuition says, "I will never tell you why. You have to find out for yourself." Then you go on a long safari in the jungle to follow where the intuition has directed. But if I refuse the intuition, then I merely arrange things. So my characters, they don't obey me. They go their own way. If they had to obey me, they would die.

The secret is that when we lift the veil of the mystery of free will versus determinism, we find a paradox. This paradox is symbolized by the two names of God used most frequently in the Torah: YHVH, the unpronounceable name of God known as the Tetragrammaton, and Elohim, the name of God that is also used to mean "judge."

YHVH, which is an amalgam of is, was, and will be, suggests that God is the absolute reality—there's nothing besides

Him. Thus, the whole story of life has to be a monologue within the Divine.

But then there's the name Elohim, representing God as the creator of human beings in His own image—God who empowered us with choice and who judges our choices. According to this truth about God, the story of life is a dialogue between human beings and God. History is a drama cowritten and produced by God and man.

Both sides of the paradox are true. Life is a monologue, predetermined and written by God. But, mysteriously, it is also a dialogue written by God and us through the free choices we make. It's beyond the either/or.

We experience the truth of this paradox. We feel, somehow, the perfection of how every scene has been written. Yet, on the other hand, we feel that we're contributing to the scene, that our choices make a difference. How can this be?

Imagine a fly walking across a painting. Although the painting is already complete, the fly has the freedom to choose how to walk across the painting. There are infinite possibilities of how that fly could explore the painting, and the fly's experience will be totally different depending on the route it takes. When it finally flies above the painting, the fly will see that there was a set picture, but its choices determined the sequence of events as it experienced them.

According to the new physics' theory of the time-space continuum, time is a dimension and all of history is as if painted on a canvas. We, however, only see a narrow portion of the whole picture. And we are free to choose how we view the picture that is already determined. Our choices create our unique and personal vision of the ultimate picture that already exists.

THE ULTIMATE CHOICE

An amazing story in the Talmud, about a Rabbi named Eliezar ben Pedat, teaches us a lot about how to play our characters and the real choices that should concern us.

Rabbi Eliezar was a very, very poor man. He subsisted on a meager diet of bread and garlic. One day, the rabbi was so hungry that he fainted. While unconscious, he had a dialogue with God. When revived by his students, he announced, "God spoke to me."

"What did He say?"

"I asked God, 'Why couldn't You create me as a rich man? Why do I have to suffer like this?' And God answered, 'Rabbi Eliezar, my dear son, would you prefer me to destroy the entire world, and re-create it, and maybe you'll be born with a different destiny?' I said, 'God, destroy the entire world? And it's only going to be a maybe? I mean it's not even for sure that I'll get a different part in this next script you write?' God replied, 'That's right.'"

Let's fathom the profundity of what this conversation is revealing. Each and every one of us is playing just the right part. And the entire world would have to be destroyed and re-created, all of history would have to be ripped up and rewritten, to attempt to give you a different part. And even after all that, there is no promise you will get a better part in the play. This is because the whole fabric of history is totally interconnected. God takes into consideration everyone's role when He writes your part. God can't just pull you out of history and write a different scene for you.

We're all part of the story. Each and every one of us with our problems, our challenges, our joys, our pain, are all written into the script, according to a vast, eternal plan.

Rabbi Eliezar ben Pedat (like many others before him and since) had asked, "Couldn't I play the rich man? Couldn't I get a different part in the script?" God's answer was that the script is so interconnected, every character is so interfaced with every other character, that to pull him out and give him a different part would mean having to rewrite the entire script.

So how did Rabbi Eliezar ben Pedat respond to this revelation? He said, "Master of the Universe, have I passed the halfway mark of my life?" God answered, "Yes, you have." Rabbi

Eliezar said, "Well, then, I'll keep my part." That's the cryptic end of the story.

What was really bothering Rabbi Eliezar ben Pedat? He was afraid that, because the part he was playing was so difficult, he wouldn't be able to play it with holiness. He was afraid that maybe he'd do something wrong. Because his poverty was so grueling, he worried that he would become bitter and take out his frustration on another person, or transgress in some other way. That's the only thing that concerned him. He didn't mind being poor. He just wanted to be good. But when God said he was past the halfway point of his life, Rabbi Eliezar saw that he was not doing so badly. He was playing his part adequately. That's all he cared about.

It's unfortunate when people are jealous because they think that somebody has a better part then they do. Every single one of us is serving God in his or her unique way. The real questions are: Do we choose to serve the Author and be a living channel bringing God into the world, or do we pretend there is no author? Do we pretend that we are the only writers of the show? Do we reject our character and try to pretend that we're someone we're not?

The human being is the only creature on earth who can be a fake. Animals are never fake. A cat never thinks that she's a dog. A cat is a cat is a cat. But a human being can confuse himself to think that he can be someone that he is not. (I admit I did see on the David Letterman show a cat that barked. I guess there's always an exception to the rule.)

When my daughter Leyadya was nine years old, her class put on a skit for the school. It was a little twenty-minute show, but to a fourth-grader it was Broadway. Leyadya came home miserable because she had been given the part of the street sweeper. She wanted to play the queen! Try to explain to a nine-year-old that playing her part well, whatever it is, is more important than having a juicy role. Unfortunately, many adults fail to learn the same lesson.

In the *Ethics of the Fathers* section of the Talmud, it is

stated: "Beloved is the man who was created in the image of God. Even more beloved is the man who knows it."

Every single character in the story is really created in the image of God, the Author, except the villain, whose job is to get all the others to express their divine image. Everyone is created in the image of God, but not everyone knows it. The joy of living is to know it, to know that it's not just my little show playing itself out in my home, with my kids and my job, but a cosmic grand epic. (After all, what part would you rather have: the lead in the school play or a small part in the next Steven Spielberg movie?)

You are great because you are part of the great drama for which God created this world. And your part, and even the particulars of your part, cannot be changed without destroying the whole world and creating it anew. And maybe not even then.

God has written the play, designed the scenes and the scenery, and determined which other people will enact the scene with you. Now, you can run away from it, or you can play your part consciously, understanding that every scene is all about the choices you make, the attitudes you adopt, the awareness you achieve, and the meaning you give to every situation.

You are free to know God and express godliness in every moment of your life. Whether it is a moment of pain or pleasure, success or failure, gain or loss, joy or sadness, you are free to choose goodness and grow.

This is the meaning of the statement in the Book of Jeremiah (9:22):

> God says, "Let not the wise man pride himself on his wisdom, nor the rich man brag about his riches, nor the strong man about his strength. Only he who knows Me, who does justice and righteousness, may take pride."

In other words, whether you are smart, rich, or strong, none of those qualities are truly your achievements that you can boast about. The real achievements of a person are the choices he or she makes. Did you choose to know God and do good? This is the only question that really matters.

Your real accomplishments do not happen on the stage of the outside world for all to see and admire. Your real accomplishments happen inside of you. They are the lessons you learn, the attitudes you adopt, and the qualities of kindness, fairness, honesty, compassion, and forgiveness that you embody.

Even if you become a big-time multimillionaire with your face on the cover of *Fortune* magazine, you still cannot take credit for your success. You are rich because God scripted you to be rich. He gave you your astute aptitude for business. He orchestrated that last-minute opening that got you into the Wharton School of Business. He set up the bizarre chance meeting with that stockbroker—when your car broke down at 2:00 a.m. on Highway 211—and He (not that stockbroker) gave you that hot tip that doubled your money. None of your big deals are really your big deals. Don't take pride in the money in your bank account. It is not the necessary results of your efforts. Any number of things could have happened to kill even your most sure deal. Your real assets in life, which are truly and forever yours, are your choices to do good and see goodness. And they are deposited within your self. They create your inner world. In the end it won't matter how much money, property, or fame you amassed for yourself in this world. What matters is not what you have but who you are. This is the only real and lasting accomplishment that is truly yours. It will go with you from this world till the next because it is you.

Even when you chose to do good but your efforts did not produce results—don't feel bad. You are not responsible for the results. Results are God's department.

We could even say that you and God are cowriters of the drama of life. But you write the choices and He writes the results. You are only responsible for the choices. The rest is in God's hands.

God writes the script for all the scenes that take place on the stage of the world at large. However, you have the sole rights to write the script of the inner world of your soul. You choose your thoughts, attitudes, perceptions, interpretations, feelings, responses, and so on. You must always remember that when you choose to be good, then you always succeed in the inner world of your soul.

Let's say you chose to raise $50,000 for an orphanage that is in dire straits, but you managed to raise only $10,000 no matter how hard you tried. Don't think that you are a failure. Your success was your good choice and your hard efforts—the rest is in God's hands.

In other words, you become good even when you simply choose to do good, although because of circumstances beyond your control you are not always able to accomplish the deed. The Talmud teaches that when a person chooses good but something prevents him from exercising his choice, his reward is the same as if he did it, because the choice is what changed him. The reward is who you become.

The Talmud also teaches that there are no rewards for the fulfillment of God's commandment in this world. This world is transient, and your accomplishments in this world are also transient. However, the rewards of fulfilling the commandments are in the inner world of your soul, which will last forever.

When you internalize these truths and live your life accordingly, you realize that in every scene of your life, God is with you. And what's important to you is not the final scene, because God already knows the final scene. What's important to you are the choices you make that determine how you will play the current scene—whether you will play it with holiness, honesty, and integrity. You want to play your role in the image of God, choosing goodness and growth.

What you *have* you can't take with you, but who you *are* is yours forever. As the saying goes, "Wherever you go, there you are." Heaven and hell are not places you go to, but states of mind that you create in yourself, the inner perceptual world of your soul. Only your choices and efforts to know God and do

His will are your responsibility and your personal success. The rest is in the hands of God. Take care not to delude yourself, overstep your boundaries, and trespass into God's domain.

That's what we learn from the story of King Hezekiah, told in the second Book of Kings. King Hezekiah was a good king of the Kingdom of Judah, an heir of the Davidic dynasty. Once he became gravely ill, and the prophet Isaiah visited him and informed him that he was going to die, and that he would not live even in the next world. At this point the Talmud takes up the story and relates the dialogue between the king and the prophet. Hezekiah asks why he would suffer such a fate. Isaiah replies that this is his punishment for failing to fulfill the commandment to be fruitful and multiply. Hezekiah explains that he did not marry and have children because he saw prophetically that one of his sons would be wicked.

God, through Isaiah, responded: "What business do you have with the secrets of the All-Merciful One?" In other words: It's none of your business if your son will turn out to be wicked. God wrote the script. Your task, Hezekiah, like everyone else's, is simply to choose to do the will of God.

Hezekiah chose to be holy, and so he didn't want to play the role of the father of a wicked son, who would succeed him on the throne and undo all the good Hezekiah had done. We can understand his reluctance to play that role. God's response, however, was that he either play his role or he's out of the play, eternally.

The "secrets of the All-Merciful One" implies that the future (which should preferably remain secret) is an outcome of God's mercy, although here in the middle of the 324th act we may not see that mercy, because we can't see the end of the drama.

Isaiah's advice to Hezekiah was that he should do what he was commanded to do, which is beget children, and let God determine the outcome. Hezekiah submitted, recovered from his illness, married Isaiah's daughter, and had a son, the wicked Menashe.

Menashe chose to be an evil king who murdered his own

grandfather, the prophet, worshiped idols, and brought destruction on the Jewish people. No one would have wanted such a rogue for a son, least of all the good Hezekiah, who had worked throughout his reign to uproot idol worship from his nation.

However, Hezekiah's job in life, like every other character in God's script, is to choose good—which also means following God's commandments. And leaving the rest up to God.

Now we can understand why the Torah prohibits all psychic and astrological means of telling the future. Our job isn't to figure out the future. The future, the development of the plot, is none of our business. To know the future would impair our ability to perfectly play the present scene. I was told that in Hollywood if a film has a death scene, they shoot the death scene first, so that the actors can relax and do the rest of the movie. Otherwise, the impending death scene would hamper them in the happy scenes. Can you imagine how hard it would be for actors to play a carefree love scene when they know that in the next scene they will be run over by a bus?

Because you do not know what will happen in the next scene, you must play the current scene as best you can. If famine strikes in Ethiopia, you cannot assume that tens of thousands of people will inevitably die. Perhaps your role is to help in organizing an international relief effort. Similarly, if you were the victim of child abuse, you cannot write off the fate of your own children on the assumption that "abused children usually grow up to be abusers." Perhaps your role is to prove the exception. The recognition of destiny cannot paralyze us from making the right choices in the present. Since the future is a secret known only to God, and the outcome of every scene is in His hands, then you write the inside story, choose the good, and transform yourself.

The Talmud teaches that King Solomon wrote the Book of Ecclesiastes after he saw prophetically that his kingdom and the Temple that he worked so hard to build would be destroyed. Imagine what a devastating realization that must have been, to know that what you invested your entire life in would be destroyed. We can understand why he bemoaned, "*Futility of futil-*

ities . . . What real value is there for a person in all his work under the sun?"

However, as we mentioned before, his ultimate resolution was *"Revere God, live by His commandments—for this is the all of man."*

King Solomon realized that our real accomplishment in life is not building the kingdom or the Temple on earth, but what we make of ourselves—the kingdom and temple we build in our inner world.

This does not mean you should not build in this world, rather that you should recognize that what you build on the outside is not the goal but the means to what you build on the inside.

The early pioneers who courageously resettled the land of Israel would often sing, "We have come to build this land and to be built by it." What is real and lasting about what you build on the outside is how it builds you and others on the inside.

When you live with this understanding, you will not be devastated when your kingdom or your temple is destroyed. You will realize that you did the will of God to build the kingdom and the temple, and even though they are destroyed, what you built inside yourself can never be destroyed. It is not as if the past was all for naught and you will have to start all over again. Rather, you now have new opportunities to continue to build yourself through the challenges and choices the destruction creates. We were not put on earth to build this world but to build ourselves in a way that expresses ourselves as the living image of God.

We can always be growing, even—and sometimes especially—when the world around us is falling apart.

Sometimes the winner is truly the loser and the loser the winner. If the winner learns nothing from his victory and doesn't grow into a better person, if he simply becomes haughty and obnoxious, then although he holds the trophy in his hands, he is actually the loser. However, if the loser accepts his loss with humbleness, overcomes feelings of anger and self-pity, and chooses to be happy with his lot, then he actually walks off with the greatest victory—an evolved self. He is the trophy.

In Summary

It's a paradox. The history of the world and your personal history are a monologue written by God . . . and yet, mysteriously, also a dialogue cowritten by God and us.

God creates the scenes, determines the plot, and orchestrates every act down to the smallest detail. However, the scene offers the characters the choice to take up the greatest opportunity to know God, to do good and be good.

The Talmud teaches that whatever happens to us is always for the best. People assume that implies that if I lose my job, an even better job is about to come my way. But I am not sure that this is always the case. Losing that great job may be for the best because the next job, which pays less and throws you into a company of very difficult people, gives you a better context for some very life-changing choices to know God and do good. In this new lousy job you will make less money but become more.

In the end, what is best is not what happens on the outside but what happens on the inside. Your choices really do make a difference, but the real difference that they make is how they change you.

5

The Divine Love Story

ONE DAY MY SON ANANIEL and my two daughters, Leyadya and Ne'ema, burst into my study. They had obviously been fighting over something and were very upset. I could see that I was chosen to be the lucky arbitrator to resolve another case of sibling rivalry. They shouted at each other, "You go, you ask Daddy." "No, no! You go, you go." Finally Ananiel, who was age five at that time, took the challenge and said, "O.K., O.K. Daddy, isn't it true that God is a boy?" Ne'ema and Leyadya, ages eight and nine, had tears in their eyes. I could hear them silently pleading with me, "Please no, please no. Tell us it's not true. It's bad enough our brother is a boy. Surely, God is really a girl." I said to them, "God is not a boy and God is not a girl. God is beyond that. We may talk about God as if He is a boy. But we really don't mean it literally." They all looked at me in shock and confusion. There was this awkward silence, and then suddenly my son blurted out, "You're wrong! He's a boy." And he stomped out of the room.

Unfortunately, many adults actually believe that God is male. And it seems from a first glance at the Book of Genesis that the Torah would agree. Throughout God is referred to as "He." Although in much of Jewish tradition we find God described as a father and king, there are references to God also as a "She," as mother or queen. However, those of us who are in the know understand that all this is holy poetry. Anything we say about God cannot be taken literally.

As we have already pointed out, according to Kabbalah, God is beyond descriptions that use neat and easy logical categories of either/or.

Let's now explore what are the masculine and feminine aspects of God.

Most people think that God is infinite. But that is incorrect. The infinite is that which goes on and on in space. However, God created space and is therefore not bound to the laws and limitation of space. If we describe God as infinite, what we really mean is that God is spaceless. *Infinite* is the opposite of *finite*, while *spaceless* means "free from the limitations of space." The One who is spaceless is free to be both beyond space and within space simultaneously. Therefore, God is beyond this finite world and yet God completely inheres every inch of the earth.

Most people think that God is eternal. But that is incorrect. Eternity would be that which goes on and on in time. But God created time and is therefore not confined to the limitations of time. If we describe God as eternal, what we really mean is that God is timeless. The eternal is the opposite of the temporal, while *timeless* means "free of the limitations of time." The One who is timeless is free to be both beyond time and within time at the same time. Therefore, God is both beyond time and yet within every moment, completely filling it with His entire presence.

And when we say that God is One, we really mean that God is nondual. One is limited; it is the opposite of many. But nonduality is free of the confines of one or many. Nonduality is free to be beyond the many and within the many. Therefore, God is beyond you, me, and everyone else in this world, and yet also within us.

How can the unlimited be expressed within the limited? How can the unlimited God be expressed within time, space, and finite beings?

If the unlimited could not be expressed within the limited, then that would be a limitation. Ultimate freedom must include the freedom to choose to be restricted. Otherwise freedom wouldn't be free; it would imply a limitation of choices—you could not choose to be restricted and limited.

This is the meaning of the kabbalistic principle called the *tzimtzum*—the divine self-restriction. Kabbalah says that God withdrew His Endless Light in order to create a place for time, space, and finite beings. God then filled time, space, and the diversity of beings with a restricted light so as not to overwhelm His creation and obliterate its existence.

Therefore, according to Kabbalah, God is free to be both beyond time and within each moment, beyond space and within every inch, beyond multiplicity and within billions of finite human beings. God is free to be manifest as one hundred percent transcendent and yet also one hundred percent immanent.

Of course, this is a contradiction and is not logical. However, we have to always be reminded that all this is from our limited point of view. From God's perspective there are not two aspects to the Divine. It is only when we describe the divine truth with our limited language that we need to speak in this paradoxical way. As one sage put it, Kabbalah is not the path to paradise but to paradox.

Metaphorically, we would say that there are two faces to the one God—the face of transcendence and the face of immanence. Kabbalah explains that the face of divine transcendence is identified with the power of masculinity and is referred to as "The Holy One, Blessed Be He." The face of divine immanence is identified with the power of femininity and is referred to as the Shekhinah—"The Divine Presence" or "The Indwelling Spirit."

In Kabbalah, masculinity is the power of rational detachment, the ability to see from outside as an objective observer. Femininity is the power to empathize, to be intimate, the ability to feel a situation from the inside, as a participant.

The Torah teaches that the first human being was created in the image of God. However, the verse that expresses this in Genesis is very strange. Here is the translation from the Soncino Press version, chapter 1, verse 27: "And God created man in His own image, in the image of God He created him; male and female He created them."

Was the first human being a "him" or a "them"? The answer is yes! The first human being was a single whole entity that included two sexes. The first human was not really male but actually beyond genders—including both male and female. The Midrash teaches that the first human had two faces—male and female. However, because the two sexes were connected back to back, they could not see each other and were not conscious of their oneness.

At a Jewish wedding ceremony, a blessing is recited that might seem puzzling: "Blessed are You, God, King of the universe, who created the human being in Your image." It might seem that this blessing would be more appropriately recited at the birth of a child than at a wedding. However, when a child is born you really do not see the full image of God. The full image of God is only manifest when the male and female unite.

Therefore, God is not male or female. God is beyond the either/or. The manifestation of God as *outside* of time, space, and finite beings is described as masculine. The manifestation of God as *within* time, space, and finite beings is described as feminine.

OPPRESSION OR EXPRESSION

The Bible speaks about God in masculine terminology, while the truth about the feminine side of God was contained in the oral tradition and revealed only to the select few. Only much later in history did the sages discuss it in public. Why?

First, because the Jewish educational tradition was designed to instill within us a clear message that God is beyond us and we are not God. If the sages had introduced the mystery of divine immanence too early to the public, they would have risked the danger of misleading people to believe that they themselves were God and that there was no significance to the boundaries and limitations of time and space. People would have fallen into the trap of pantheism.

Human beings needed to first firmly understand that God is beyond them before they could be introduced to the truth that God is also manifest within them.

There is also a moral reason why Jewish tradition talks about God predominantly in the male gender. One of the objectives of the Torah is to guide humanity and empower us with making the choices that express our holiness and liberate our true inner self, the Divine within. This, however, cannot be accomplished until we subdue our selfish, egotistical inclinations and tame some of our lustful animal drives.

Therefore, the Torah directs and disciplines us toward submission and obedience to God, the King—the transcendental God. However, this is only in order to help us access and express our true selves—the Divine within, the Queen. Ironically, after a while, our submission and obedience to God as the power beyond us transforms us and becomes an expression of our freedom, an ecstatic experience of the manifestation of God as the essential power within us.

Initially, we hear the voice of a transcendental God who commands us to obey. However, after we submit and obey, eventually we hear this same voice, but now it is coming not from outside but from within us. It is as if the divine voice that we heard speaking *to* us is now also speaking *through* us. We are now tuned in to the voice of God speaking through our soul, which is really a spark of God. Then the commandments are no longer acts of obedience but rather the free expression of our true inner self.

In other words, after we obey God's will we discover that this is actually what we *want* because our true inner will is really an aspect of God's will.

The Talmud reports two opposite opinions about what will be the status of the commandments when the Messiah comes. One sage taught that in the future the commandments will be annulled, as they will no longer be needed, while another sage taught that in the future the commandments will still apply. There is no contradiction here. In the future, mankind will continue to fulfill the commandments, only not as acts of obedience to the transcendental God, not as *commandments*, but as the natural expression of who we are—souls, or sparks of God.

Kabbalah teaches that when we do not adhere to the commandments, it is as if we are divorcing the manifestation of the Divine within (the Shekhinah) from the manifestation of the Divine beyond (the "Holy One, Blessed Be He"). However, when we obey the commandments, then we are uniting the manifestation of the Divine within us with the manifestation of the Divine beyond us. We are like a switch that can either break the circuit that reveals God's mysterious oneness (that is both beyond and within the many) or connect the circuit. Therefore, Kabbalah instructs us to recite before the performance of a commandment: "For the purpose of uniting the Holy One, Blessed Be He, and the Shekhinah. . . ."

It is through our human choices that this unification is revealed. Our job is to acknowledge the unity of the two aspects of the one God—transcendence and immanence—through freely choosing to obey God's command. This is exactly what "choosing to do what we must do" is all about. What we must do comes upon us as a command from outside. What we choose is our choice from within. When we choose to do what we must do, we reveal the unity of the Divine within us with the Divine beyond us. We then feel connected and an incredible energy of life force and awareness flows through us.

Once again I remind you to please be careful, because we are treading on dangerous ground here. We do not unify "parts" of God. God has no parts and is already absolutely one. Our spiritual work and accomplishments are only epistemological (that is, a matter of our perceptions) and not ontological (a matter of reality).

God is one, was one and always will be one. However, this oneness is hidden and not perceived, recognized, or experienced by us. This is the meaning of Zechariah's prophetic description of the future redemption. "And on that day God will be one and His name will be one"(14:9). God is one right now, today, but people do not see, acknowledge, or experience that truth.

It is as if we had a temporary problem with our eyes and suffered from double vision. Our problem is not with *what* we are looking at but with the *way* we are looking—the way that we perceive. Zechariah teaches us that right now God is one but His name is not one. We do not yet recognize and perceive God's oneness. For us, it is hidden. However, in the future we will perceive God's oneness. We will perceive and acknowledge that His name is "One." Therefore, history is actually an evolution of consciousness—an adventure in awareness toward the realization and recognition of God's oneness, which is the ultimate experience of love.

SPIRITUAL SEXUALITY

There are many sexual allusions in Kabbalah regarding the various stages in the process of consciousness, unifying, so to speak, the male and female manifestations of God. Words like *kissing, hugging,* and *intercourse* are common in kabbalistic works. This is one of the reasons why only mature people should study Kabbalah. Otherwise, these holy sexual metaphors could be easy desecrated. I must admit that as I write these ideas I feel great trepidation. I pray that you will treat these matters with great sensitivity and much reverence. They can be easily misunderstood and abused.

These sexual allusions all suggest that the theme of life is a gradual process toward the realization of God's oneness—the ultimate experience of love. There is at all times a holy and cosmic spiritual sexuality at play. Our choice is whether or not we participate in it by choosing to be vehicles for it.

As I have already mentioned, all this is only from our perspective. It is only a way to understand as best as we can what life is all about, and what our role in it is. From God's perspective there is only oneness. There is never a separation between the transcendental and the immanent. There is always and only simple oneness. However, the question is whether that oneness is conscious or not.

This is the hidden message behind the story of the creation of the first human being. As we have noted, Adam was originally a single entity with two faces—male and female. However, the two sides were connected back to back. God said "It is not good that Adam is alone. I will make for him a helper who is opposite and equal to him." God then brought animals to Adam to see what he would call them. However, Adam did not find a mate among them and was saddened. God then put him to sleep, and according to Kabbalah and Talmud, split Adam in half, separating the male side from the female side. God then brought them face to face.

Although Adam was originally one being, she/he was not aware of the true meaning of this mysterious oneness. Once she/he was split into two, she/he/they were able to face each other and choose to become one, achieve consciousness of true oneness, and experience the ecstasy of love.

This story is a metaphor for the cosmic story of life and hints at the purpose of creation. It teaches us that we all have a role in a cosmic drama whose theme is the process of divine self-knowledge. In this process, oneness becomes conscious and is experienced and expressed as love.

God is one. However, does God know that She/He is one? Does God experience His/Her oneness? Does God have the choice to become one? The answer is yes and no. The answer is beyond the either/or of our logical minds. Our mission in life is not to understand this profound truth but to facilitate it, live it, experience it, and celebrate it. Our mission is to acknowledge the oneness and reveal the love. Our mission is to realize that we are in essence one with each other and one with God. Our challenge is to realize that only love is real.

The Book of Proverbs (16:4) teaches that all that God created, He created for Himself. However, the Book of Psalms (89:3) teaches that the creation of the world is founded upon loving-kindness. Was creation selfish or selfless? The answer is beyond the either/or. The answer is love. Love is beyond the either/or of selfish or selfless. According to Kabbalah, God is one and we—despite the illusion of our separateness from God and from each other—are, in fact, included within God's oneness and permeated by God's oneness. The light surrounds the vacuum and yet fills it. Our task is to become conscious of this truth and to live it by choosing to love each other and to love God.

The true power of human sexuality is actually rooted in the cosmic process of *spiritual* sexuality. There is an urge to merge and reveal oneness. This is why it is so potent and must be approached with great holiness. According to Jewish tradition, when sex is a true expression of love, it is the "holy of holies."

According to Kabbalah, if God is not in your bedroom, sex will be boring. True sexual fulfillment comes only when sex is part of a spiritual service—a vehicle for the expression of divine oneness—true love. Only then is it connected to the cosmic circuit of divine self-knowledge—the ultimate realization of timeless love. Sexuality without love is not true intimacy, and it will never reach the sublime heights of ecstasy.

God's Mirror

When the Book of Genesis declares that God created man in His image, it is telling us what life is all about. The pagans engraved images of gods in stone and wood, but this is telling us that our real task is to be a *living* reflection of God's image.

A person who is an expression and reflection of God is truly serving God.

In the Torah, God actually commands us to "walk" in His ways. The sages interpret this commandment as meaning that we should emulate the divine attributes such as mercy, kindness, generosity, and dependability by visiting the sick, consoling the mourners, fulfilling our promises, and developing positive character traits. A person who actually cultivates such traits and expresses them in concrete actions has made himself or herself into a reflection of the Divine. Our goal as human beings is to choose love and become, so to speak, a mirror for God.

But how can we possibly do that?

This is exactly what the Torah is all about: it tells us how.

The commandments of the Torah, which come to us through divine revelation, enable us to actualize the divine image that we were created to be and thereby reflect the attributes of God, connect the circuit of God's self-knowledge, and experience love.

That's why my behavior can't be dictated by me alone; it must be guided by God. Outside the framework of the commandments, even the most exalted human wisdom, the highest spiritual practices formulated by the most enlightened master, cannot enable me to tap into and complete the circuit of divine self-knowledge and love.

The truth is that the urge within us to find God is actually coming from God (as we will see in the next chapter). Somehow we are participants in a process of divine self-knowledge and love. Each and every one of us is a character in a drama written by the Great Author to be a vehicle for His own process of self-reflection and realization. Our choice is whether we consciously play this role, whether we choose to mirror God and reflect back to God the light of true oneness. God's self-expression and our reflecting back to God His truth are referred to in Kabbalah respectively as the "direct light" and the "reflected light."

Each character in the drama can choose to reflect the light of God and connect the circuit of divine self-knowledge and love. This is what it really means to serve God—to contribute in facilitating this divine process, whereby the One becomes conscious through free choice and is experienced as love. That is why the significance of our choices is measured not by how we affect what is going on around us, but what happens within us. The focus of our choices is not about how to change the world but how to change ourselves and achieve a higher awareness of God's truth. This is our only goal and true accomplishment in life. Remember what God said in the book of the prophet Jeremiah: "Only he who knows Me, who does justice and righteousness, may take pride." This is also the message of the verse in Proverbs (3:6): "In all your ways know Him."

However, the process does not start with us and does not end with us. As the Book of Isaiah (44:6) reveals: "I am God, I am the first and I am the last, and there is no god [no other power] but Me."

From the character's perspective, he is the subject and the story is about him. It starts with him and it ends with him. But from the perspective of the Author, He is the subject, and the whole story is only about Him. The character is the vehicle for the Author's process of self-expression and reflection. The character's true meaning in life is achieved by serving as a means for the Author's life. The character's ultimate fulfillment is to experience the Author.

Our service to God is to connect the circuit of God's own self-reflection and realization—the experience of love. Our greatest reward is the very opportunity to participate and facilitate this inner divine process. The reward of love is love. This process is hinted at in King Solomon's magnificent Song of Songs, which is referred to in the Talmud as the "Holy of Holies"—the one Holy that mysteriously includes many Holies. And this is true love, a oneness that includes many and yet remains one (like the one Adam who included the two sexes).

The drama we are playing out is history. It is an adventure in consciousness. It doesn't start with us and it doesn't end with us. It is all about God. We all intuit that our life has no meaning or fulfillment unless it is a means to a greater end beyond our self. This is the path of the commandments that direct us in our service of the Great Self—God. (For more on this subject, see my book *Endless Light,* chapter 7.)

Our role in this drama is to take up the task as articulated in the Book of Deuteronomy (4:39): "You shall know this day and take into your heart that the Lord is God in the heaven above and upon the earth below, there is nothing else."

The climax of this drama will happen when all the characters finally take up this responsibility—and this is when the prophecy of Zechariah will be fulfilled: "And on that day, God will be one and His name will be one." And then we will realize that life was not my story or your story—it was His-story.

History is God's autobiography, self-published, for an exclusive market: God. It's written by God, about God, for the sake of God. There is no way to buy a copy of this autobiography and put it on our shelves. But we can identify ourselves as characters in the story. We can have a role in God's autobiography. We can choose to overcome evil, do good, love, and become conscious and meaningful characters in His story.

HISTORY OR HER-STORY

Kabbalah is a Hebrew word that means "to receive," but it also means "parallel." One of the main principles of Kabbalah is that the microcosm reflects the macrocosm. Therefore, the dynamics of our individual lives mirror the dynamics of the cosmic life. The story of Adam and Eve in the Garden of Eden, however, not only parallels the cosmic process as I just explained but also represents the repeating pattern of life.

Adam and Eve were living a carefree life in the Garden of Eden. They had only one restriction. God commanded them not to eat of the Tree of Knowledge of Good and Bad. However, forbidden fruits tend to seem more tasty to people. In addition, having a seductive snake around encouraging them to eat it made the challenge all the more difficult.

This part of the story most people are familiar with. However a little less familiar is what the snake really said to them to lure them into the sin. The snake did not say, "Hey, you know what? God doesn't want you to eat from that tree because He knows that the day you eat from it, you'll be rich." The snake knew that deep down inside, people are not really motivated by wealth; it's not money they want. The snake also did not seduce them by telling them that they would become famous. Fame does not attract people either. And the snake did not even use sex as bait. He did not claim that the forbidden fruit would give them a great sex life. According to the Torah sex really has no appeal to human beings. In other words, this story is teaching us that wealth, fame, or sex cannot really seduce people into doing wrong. They are just counterfeits to what we really want to accomplish. The snake knew what was the true desire of human beings. The snake said, "God does not want you to eat of that tree because if you do, then you too will be like God." Now, that is appealing!

The snake knew the human secret, but he was seducing Adam and Eve into a counterfeit of the real thing.

According to the Torah, the root of all drives and ambitions of humanity is to be divine. Wealth, fame, and sexual pleasure appeal to us only as accoutrements of this most basic drive to be all-powerful and Godlike. But they do not fulfill our genuine inner desires.

This story is teaching us that in the depths of our souls we want to be who we are. Because our true inner selves are actually a manifestation of divine immanence, we want to achieve the status of being a god. Therefore, even when we do wrong, it is in an effort to claim our right to be our own god. That's what's wrong about it. We are created in the *image* of God, but we are not gods.

All we want to achieve in our lives is to be who we are. True freedom is the freedom to be true to ourselves. I want to be free to be me. The manifestation of divine immanence is bursting forth from within me, seeking to be expressed.

This was the underlying dilemma of Adam and Eve. In effect, they had to ask themselves: "Do we surrender our freedom and obey God, or do we affirm ourselves and do what we want?" They didn't realize that the answer is not either/or—it is yes and yes.

Our challenge is to realize that the very power within us is completely one with the power beyond us. When we obey and surrender to the voice of God commanding us from without, we actually give expression and affirmation to the voice of God within us. This is the irony, mystery, and ecstasy of divine oneness. Suddenly we experience our surrender of self as an affirmation of self. Our surrender to God beyond us actually reveals that aspect of God within us—the soul.

It is like running your finger along a Möbius strip—a continuous one-sided surface that can be formed from a rectangular strip by rotating one end 180 and attaching it to the other end. At first you are on the outside, and then you mysteriously find yourself on the inside. But when you continue forward, you again find yourself on the outside.

Adam and Eve did not understand this. They thought that they could establish and affirm their true selves by defying the command of God. However, when they boldly defied the will of God, rather than feeling empowered by this courageous affirmation of self, they suddenly felt weak and scared. Before this act of defiance, they felt comfortable in the presence of God, but afterward they hid. In other words, their affirmation of self in defiance of the will of God actually ended up as a surrender of self—a loss of self.

Kabbalah explains that Adam and Eve divorced the Shekhinah from the "Holy One, Blessed Be He." They separated the manifestation of divine immanence from the manifestation of divine transcendence. This is the dynamic of *all* wrongdoing. When we divorce the Divine "within" from the Divine "beyond," then our innermost self is dwarfed. It is severed from its source and uprooted from its ground. Not only can we not face God, but our self-esteem is severely diminished.

According to the metaphor of Kabbalah, when the manifestation of divine immanence is disconnected from the manifestation of divine transcendence, the Shekhinah Herself no longer faces and reflects the greatness of divine transcendence—the Holy One, Blessed Be He—and thereby shrinks in stature.

Kabbalah teaches that the light of the moon symbolizes the light of divine immanence, and the light of the sun symbolizes the light of divine transcendence. The ideal relationship, figuratively speaking, is when the sun and the moon are face to face. Then the light of the moon is a bright and full reflection of the light of the sun. However, when the moon is not face to face with the sun, then its light is diminished down to a fraction.

Kabbalah teaches that originally the light of the moon was as bright as the sun. However, after Adam and Eve ate from the Tree of Knowledge in defiance of God's commandment, the light of the moon was diminished. In the messianic age the light of the moon will be restored and will shine as full and bright as the sun. This will happen when humanity returns to God and the consciousness of God will fill the earth as the water fills the oceans. In other words, the mysterious oneness of God that is beyond and within time, space, and humanity will be experienced and consciously realized by all.

When you read the Torah in the light of Kabbalah, you discover that it is less about His-story and more about Her-story. The star of the show is the evolving stature of the Shekhinah and Her return to the ultimate face-to-face union with the "Holy One, Blessed Be He." Please, please, remember that this is all epistemological (a matter of perception), not ontological (a matter of reality).

The Torah shows how Adam and Eve intuit the manifestation of the Shekhinah within them and mistakenly seek to establish themselves as gods by defying God. In so doing, they actually achieve the opposite. In pulling themselves away from God, they lose their connection to the Divine Source of all self-esteem and can no longer face God. The theme of the Torah, then, is the progression of humanity in its struggle to rebuild the stature of the Shekhinah (our innermost divine source of self-esteem) and achieve face-to-face union with the "Holy One, Blessed Be He."

The redemption of *all* of humanity is described as the redemption of the Shekhinah. In practical terms, this means that in the time of redemption, we will no longer suffer the curse of male dominance: "And he will rule over her"(Genesis 3:16). We will no longer think that God is only "male," only transcendent. We will understand that God is beyond the either/or of transcendence versus immanence. God is one. And we are one with God, although not the same as God. This oneness is the wonder of true love.

Forgive me for repeating myself, but remember that this process of redemption is only epistemological—it is only a process of consciousness and experience. Ontologically, God was, is, and will always be one and only. But the process is about oneness becoming conscious.

When Adam and Eve took a bite out of the forbidden fruit, they separated the Shekhinah from the Holy One, Blessed Be He, diminished Her stature, and brought upon the world the curse of male dominance. The male aspect of God—divine transcendence—then became predominant. (This set the stage for monotheism, which is explained in chapter 7.) His-story started with the eating of the forbidden fruit and continued with Cain killing his brother Abel. It then proceeded with a series of crimes and culminated with the destruction of the world during the time of Noah.

Her-story started when Abraham obeyed the command of God to "go for yourself," and continued when Abraham began to reestablish the divine source of human self-esteem through a relationship with God.

Until Abraham, people were stuck in the either/or mode of thinking. They either believed that they were gods or believed they were nothing. In other words, they believed either that Divinity was completely within them and they were divine, or that Divinity was completely beyond them and they were nothing.

Divine immanence and Divine transcendence were mutually exclusive terms.

This seems to be the story of all religious and political philosophies. Humanity is on a seesaw, bouncing up and down from one extreme to another. Either the Divine is perceived to be within us, and therefore the individual is all that matters and is free to do as he or she pleases; or the Divine is beyond humanity, and the individual must sacrifice everything for the greater whole.

Abraham, however, set the cornerstone for a new way—beyond either/or. His was the way of oneness, the art of loving.

Kabbalah tells us that Abraham and Sarah set the process in motion for the redemption of the Shekhinah. This process continues to play itself out through the efforts of Isaac, Rebecca, Jacob, Rachel, Leah, and Jacob's twelve sons. They, however, only succeeded in redeeming the Shekhinah for themselves as individuals. The redemption of the Shekhinah still had to be accomplished on a national level. This process begins with the liberation of the nation of Israel from slavery in Egypt and progresses with the collective revelation of the Torah at Mount Sinai when the entire nation met God face to face. (As Moses relates in Deuteronomy 5:4: "Face to face, God spoke with you [the nation of Israel] at the mountain from within the fire.")

The culmination of national redemption happens when the Jewish people return to the Promised Land and rebuild the Holy Temple in Jerusalem.

This, however, is not enough, because the ultimate redemption must be universal—reaching the entire world. Therefore, the finale of this great "love story" is the coming of the messiah, who will negotiate world peace and inspire universal love. Then the awareness of the mysterious divine oneness and the ecstasy of love will embrace and fill all. "Then the knowledge of God will fill the earth as the waters fill the seas" (Isaiah 11:9). Love and peace will reign supreme.

This is what the world is waiting for. On the wall outside the General Assembly headquarters in New York City, the United

Nations has chosen to borrow the words of the Jewish prophet Isaiah to express this ultimate vision:

> *And they shall beat their swords into plowshares and their spears into pruning hooks. Nations shall not lift up sword against nations. Neither shall they learn war anymore.* [Isaiah 2:4]

However, as good as this sounds, this is not the ultimate end. Peace, brotherhood, and love are not a destiny; they are a never-ending journey. The joyous consciousness of God's oneness—the experience of love—will grow forever.

THE NATURE OF MIRACLES, THE MIRACLES OF NATURE

Will all this happen through some outrageous miracle?

The answer is no, and to explain how that is so, we need to delve into the nature of miracles.

People often say, "If there is really a God, why doesn't He do miracles anymore? I would believe in God if I saw the sea split or some other supernatural event."

This question comes from a "male" orientation to God. God, the Miracle Worker, is part of His-story but not so much part of Her-story. In the past, God did miracles in order to prevent some terrible tragedy from happening. God overruled the laws of nature to keep the story going—otherwise, it would have ended. But this type of intervention is not the ideal way that God wants to act. God prefers not to do miracles. He only does them when there is no other way to keep the story going or to show His control of nature.

People do not really change by witnessing a miracle. Of course, at first they are strongly moved and seem to change. But the awe quickly wears off, and they return to their old ways. We see this human pattern many times in the stories of the Torah.

The Israelites witnessed the miraculous splitting of the sea and were saved from destruction at the hands of the Egyptian armies. However, not too long afterward, their faith deteriorated, and they began to complain about their conditions in the desert. Miracles don't change people, only people can change themselves; and to accomplish that, they have to make choices and get proactive.

There is another reason why God is reluctant to do miracles. And that is because the story of life is Her-story. The star of the show is the evolving manifestation of God's spirit within humanity. Miracles actually stifle the growth of the expression of the Shekhinah from within us. The light of divine immanence must evolve through our choices, our commitments, and our hard work.

This explains the bizarre behavior of the Israelites who wrestled with the significance of their identity in the desert for forty years. The desert was a miraculous place for the Israelites. They enjoyed a daily portion of manna, the heavenly bread that fell daily from the sky. They also drank water that flowed abundantly from a rock. For forty years the Israelites sojourned in a miraculous desert where everything was upside down. Generally wheat comes from the ground and water from the skies, but for forty years it was just the opposite.

In the desert the Israelites lived in a divine womb, like a fetus whose needs are completely cared for. And yet with all these comforts they complained and rebelled over and over again. Why?

Because under these miraculous conditions, their inner stature was dwarfed. It was like you and I living under the shadow of our parents. There is a spirit within us that is restless and demands to be established and expressed. This spirit is the manifestation of the Divine within us that must evolve and emerge. This is why the miraculous desert was not the destination of the Israelites. It was only part of their process and journey.

Their original destination was the Promised Land. The funny thing, though, is that when they were about to get there, they started to have second thoughts. They sent in a group of spies to check it out. This group returned after a quick look and told the people that the Promised Land consumes its inhabitants. In other words, it was a place that demands a lot of work. The people wondered, "Why should we leave the comfortable womb of God that encompasses us with daily miracles? Why leave this wonderful desert and go to a land that demands so much human effort and hard work? What is so promising about the Promised Land?"

This was their dilemma: On the one hand, the divine spirit within them wanted to become manifest through their choices, determined efforts, and hard work. Therefore, they resented all the freebies in the desert. But then again, it was also very nice to have it all miraculously handed to them on a silver platter and to bask in the light of God. Why should they soil themselves with the labors of this physical world when they could stay in bliss and enjoy the supernatural desert? Why leave the spiritual life of the desert and go to work?

Essentially, this story captures the real identity crisis of all of humanity: "Is God within us or beyond us?" Are we part of His-story, witnessing how God from above snaps His fingers, abrogates the laws of nature, and does miracles? Or are we part of Her-story, serving as a vehicle for the manifestation of the aspect of God within, seeking to participate in a process of becoming, expressed through our struggles, our choices, and our efforts?

Once again the answer is yes and yes.

The forty years in the desert was a time for the revelation of the face of God's transcendence, showing that God is the Power who is above and beyond the laws and limitations of nature. During that time the Israelites developed a profound belief in divine transcendence—God was manifest as the Holy One, Blessed Be He. And they understood that they were not God. But then the time came for the manifestation of the face of divine immanence—that aspect of God which is expressed from within humanity.

These are the two faces of the one and only God.

The problem with the miraculous life in the desert was that the light of divine transcendence eclipsed the light of divine immanence. But the danger in the Promised Land was that the light of divine immanence could eclipse the light of divine transcendence. In the Promised Land, the Israelites could come to think that all their success was really their own and had nothing to do with God.

The dilemma of the Israelites just before they entered into the Promised Land sheds light on our own dilemma today. Every day we witness amazing advancements in science and technology. We, too, are creators of worlds. We seem to be ascending to the stature of gods. Will we let this power go to our heads and fool us into thinking that we are gods and do as we please? Or do we humbly accept these powers as gifts from God, signs of the growing light of the Divine within? Do we choose to do what we must do, humbly obey and follow God's commandments, and thereby connect the light of the Divine within with the light of the Divine beyond?

Do we delude ourselves and think that life is *our* story, or do we rise to the ultimate realization that it is all really His/Her story and that our joy is to serve?

IN SUMMARY

So is God male or female? By now you know the answer. The complete image of God is the oneness of love—beyond the either/or. We are all part of a divine adventure in consciousness, whether we choose to know it or not. However, our greatest joy is to know it. Every thought we think, every word we say, and every act we do can be like a wire that connects or disconnects the currents of consciousness uniting the divine lights—beyond and within.

Our challenge is to choose love and experience the ecstatic mystery of God's oneness. We achieve true happiness when we choose to complete the circuit of God's self-refection and knowledge; and let the light of love glow. This is our work, and this is our reward.

6

Hide and Seek

IN ORDER TO EXPLAIN some deep kabbalistic truths, the great eighteenth-century Hasidic master Rebbe Nachman of Breslov was fond of telling stories. In his story "The Humble King," he metaphorically illustrates the process of the divine self-reflection and knowledge.

A king summons his adviser and tells him that he has portraits of all of the kings of the world except one, which, of course, he must have to complete his collection. He charges his adviser to locate this king and draw his portrait. However, this is not such a simple task. No one has ever seen this king, because he sits behind a curtain. Another mysterious thing—this king signs himself "the mighty warrior, man of truth, and humble person." (If the story sounds somewhat familiar, keep in mind that Rebbe Nachman died about ninety years before the book *The Wizard of Oz* was written.)

The wise adviser accepts his mission and goes to the country where the mysterious king rules. In order to garner clues on how to approach the king, he decides to get to know the land first. He goes about this in a strange way—by listening to jokes the populace tells. He reasons that the essential nature of a country lies in its sense of humor. From their jokes, the adviser comes to understand that the citizens of this land are false and deceitful.

With that knowledge under his belt, the adviser devises a way to see the king. He enters into a business deal and allows himself to be cheated. Then he takes his case to court, where he finds that the court itself operates by bribery and falsehood. So he takes his case to a higher court, where he encounters the same corruption. He takes his case to successively higher courts until he can finally bring it before the king, who is adjudicating cases from behind a curtain.

When the adviser is finally granted an audience, he tells the king that his kingdom is completely filled with falsehood.

Now, logically we might expect the king to be just like his subjects. But the adviser thinks maybe this is not so; maybe the king is really a man of truth, and that is why he conceals himself—to distance himself from his subjects because he cannot tolerate their lies.

With that thought in mind, the adviser starts praising the king, to see whether he's truly humble, and as he praises the king more and more, the king becomes smaller and smaller, until he becomes almost as if nothing. Finally, the king pulls open the curtains to see who is this man who understands him so well. At that moment the adviser quickly draws a picture of the king, which he brings back to his own monarch.

This story full of kabbalistic allusions is unusual because it has two kings; generally Rebbe Nachman's stories have one king, who symbolizes God. It's bizarre that in this story one king is sending his adviser to find another king. Who's the other king? There really isn't another king. This story is about two aspects of one king.

Rebbe Nachman is teaching us that the one who has sent you on your quest is the one you're looking for. The king beyond us is sending us to find the king within us. The king beyond us, so to speak, wants to see a picture of the king within us—which is really a reflection of himself. The adviser represents each and every one of us. Our challenge and journey in life is to paint the unique portrait of the king within us as a reflection of the king beyond us. Each of us must express and reveal the uniqueness of our soul as a reflection of God. The mission of the king's adviser (you and me) is to be the king's (God's) agent and work on His behalf to facilitate His process of self-reflection and knowledge. In other words, our mission from God is to become the unique image of God that we were created to become and to reflect God's truth. But the journey means having to go to a far-off land of lies, which is this world. This world deludes us to think that the two kings are far and removed from each other. This is the world of either/or where divine transcendence and divine immanence seem separate and contradictory. This is also a world of lies where the truth of the godliness within us is hidden from us.

In a world of either/or, there is no love and respect, because it is every person for him- or herself. God's oneness is hidden, and there is no understanding of the true meaning of love. People do not respect the godliness within each other and are blind to God's pervasive oneness that should inspire love between them. Therefore, the adviser discovers that in this land everyone is cheating and deceiving each other.

He intuits that in order to succeed in his mission he needs to understand the humor of the country. Humor is the necessary key to handle the daily challenges of life and advance forward on this journey. According to Kabbalah, you can only gain true wisdom through humor—which comes from a place higher than logic. On a spiritual journey, you must be able to laugh and not take the challenges on the way too seriously. You may think that the obstacles are trying to stop you from reaching your goal, but actually they are contributing to your ultimate success and enhancing your appreciation of the goal when you get there. Adam and Eve would have needed a good sense of humor in order to realize that the snake really did not want them to eat from the tree; he was only challenging them so that they would realize their love for God. We explained earlier, in chapter 4, that evil is like a prostitute who has been hired by a king to challenge his son and thereby offer him the opportunity to become conscious of who he is and his relationship to his father. The prostitute is really working for the king and does not want the son to fall to temptation. If we were to see a person trying very hard to persuade people to do something, but we knew all along that he really did not want them to do it, we would find it humorous.

Humor also requires objectivity. On a spiritual journey, a good sense of humor helps you avoid taking your perspective too seriously. This enables you to handle the apparent incongruities, which come from seeing only part of the whole picture. When people can laugh at a situation, it means they are not too involved. They can get beyond their take on the situation and see it within a greater context, from a higher perspective.

There is a story about Rabbi Akiva, one of the greatest leaders in Jewish history, who lived around the time of the destruction of the Holy Temple by the Romans in 70 CE. The sight of the Temple of Jerusalem in ruins caused the sages to weep with despair. Only Rabbi Akiva laughed. How could he laugh at one of the worst calamities ever to befall the Jewish people? Rabbi Akiva explained: his joyful laughter sprang from the realization that just as the prophesied destruction of the Temple came true, so too the biblical prophecy of its reconstruction and the coming of the glorious age of the Messiah will surely occur.

Rabbi Akiva had the ability to get beyond the moment and see it within the larger picture of God's plan. The contrast between the dismal moment and the bright future (which the moment was actually a conduit for) was humorous to him.

The messianic age is described in Psalms 126 as a time when "our mouths will be filled with laughter." All the horrible and conflicting events of history will fall into place. We will get a panoramic view of all time—past, present, and future—and we will burst into laughter. We will see how all the challenges and darkest times of history were precisely what brought about the light.

The adviser had to keep his sense of humor to finally find the king. He needed a sense of humor to understand the real joke: that the king was hiding not because he didn't want the adviser to find him—the king was hiding so that he would be found.

The One in the Many, the Many in the One

What is God hiding?

Himself—His oneness.

To understand this, we need first to explore the profound meaning of God's true oneness. The oneness of God is not like the oneness in our dictionary. It's not like the number one. Many people who don't understand Torah say, "What's the big obsession with God being one? Western culture stopped believing in many gods thousands of years ago."

But the oneness of God does not mean that He is only one as opposed to two or three. The oneness of God is an all-encompassing unity that includes multiplicity while remaining one. The light surrounds the vacuum and yet fills it. It's a mysterious oneness. The *Sefer Yetzirah* (Book of Formation), a kabbalistic classic, asks: "Before the number one, what do you count? Such is the Divine."

In another classic, *Tikkunei Zohar* (Embellishments on the *Zohar*), the Prophet Elijah is quoted as saying, "Master of the Universe You are one, but not in number."

As we explained before, the oneness of God is nondual; it is not the opposite of "many"—not simply one of a pair of opposites, but rather beyond the duality of opposites. It is thus a oneness that includes both one and many. The closest experience we have that delivers to us a taste of God's oneness is love. In love, two can be one and yet two. It is a wonderful (one-derful) mystery.

When God's oneness is concealed, we see many separate forces, many independent people, many disparate situations, many isolated objects. We may even think there is no God and no ultimate oneness, that there is just us in this fragmented world of chaos.

In truth, however, the One is in the many, and the many are in the One. But when that oneness is hidden, all that we see is fragmentation and multiplicity. And we live in a world that encourages attitudes of selfishness, deceit, hate, competition, and warfare.

However when we ascend into the higher worlds of perception (as I will soon explain), where the truth of God's oneness is revealed, then we realize that only love is real and everything else is an illusion.

From whom is God hiding His oneness?

From the soul. From you and me.

However, Kabbalah describes the soul as a spark of God. Therefore, God is, so to speak, hiding Himself from an aspect of Himself. The godliness within us is yearning to find and reconnect with the godliness beyond us. And the godliness beyond us is yearning to find and reconnect with the godliness within us. As we mentioned earlier, this is what's called in Kabbalah the yearning to unify the light of divine transcendence (the Holy One, Blessed Be He) with the light of divine immanence (the Shekhinah).

To "reconnect" is the real purpose of any authentic religion. The word *religion* comes from the Latin *religare,* which means "to reconnect," and which shares its root with *ligament* (which connects two bones).

Of course, we are never really disconnected, but as long as God's oneness is hidden, we think we are and we feel we are. To change this feeling, we must consciously re-connect; we must change our mind-set.

Life is a journey in consciousness. In truth, God is always one and we are always one with God and with each other. The problem is that we don't know that truth. This is a critical point. We are always one with the ultimate—our work is to achieve an *awareness* of that truth. This awareness is the ecstatic experience of ultimate love.

This helps us understand the true meaning of the commandment "Love your neighbor as yourself" (Leviticus 19:18).

How can we be commanded to have feelings of love toward another person? What if we simply have nothing in common? What if we seriously disagree over many political and social issues? How can we be expected to love people who are so different from ourselves?

The commandment is actually telling us that in reality we are already one, and we *can* definitely experience that to be true and feel the love. However, to achieve this realization we must act in ways that express and reveal that truth. This is the theme of all the commandments dealing with interpersonal relationships.

This is the same dynamic behind the commandment to love God. We are already one with God. But we need to acknowledge that in what we think, say, and do. Then we will feel it. This is the theme of all the commandments dealing with our relationship to God.

WORLDS APART

So why, then, do we feel separate from God and from each other? Why is this oneness not obvious? What hides God's oneness? Why do we see so much chaos?

Because of the world—or, to be more precise, the worlds.

The Hebrew word for world is *olam*, which derives from a root word meaning to disappear or to be concealed. An *olam* is a dimension of concealment, a dimension of hiddenness. In most Jewish prayers, we refer to God as *Melekh ha-Olam*, which is usually translated as "King of the Universe," but it also suggests "The King of Hiddenness." God is the King of Hiddenness.

According to Kabbalah, there are four worlds, which reflect

four levels of consciousness. These worlds are not like separate planets, one above the other, but rather like concentric circles one within the other. The lowest world is the most external and conceals the most. The highest world in the most internal and most revealed.

The lowest world is referred to as the world of action, *asiyyah*. The next up is called the world of *yetzirah*, formation. The next is *beriyah,* the world of creation. The highest world, which we generally don't talk about (because it is beyond words), is called *atzilut*, the world of emanation.

Atzilut	World of Emanation
Beriyah	World of Creation
Yetzirah	World of Formation
Asiyyah	World of Action

Thus, the very term *worlds* indicates various levels and dimensions of hiddenness. Since we're in the lowest world, the dimension of the greatest hiddenness and concealment, we don't see God's oneness. We look around our world, and we see multiplicity and separateness.

Visualize yourself at, say, the departure gate of an airport. What do you see? A couple of hundred separate individuals. But if you were to ascend to the higher realms of consciousness, then you would become aware how, although all these individuals are in some sense distinct, they are not separate but essentially one. God's oneness actually embraces and permeates everyone and everything. The light surrounds the vacuum and yet completely fills it. However, God is hiding His oneness.

Each world (or dimension) is a graduated level of hiddenness, so that the lower we descend, the more hidden God becomes. Since we humans live in the lowest world, the world of

action, the ultimate truth and the ultimate experience of love is
most hidden to us. As we ascend to the world of formation, a
little more is revealed. And as we reach the world of creation,
even more is revealed.

God has hidden himself from us through these worlds so
well that, in this lowest world that we live in, we almost begin
to believe that maybe there isn't a God. Maybe there's just us.
Maybe there is just a multiplicity and diversity of unrelated separate independent beings. Maybe there is just chaos.

Wouldn't it be better if everything was just right out in the
open? What's the point of this hiddenness?

To answer this question, we must first be clear what it means
to hide from someone. When I'm hiding from you, where am I?
I'm right here. You just don't see me. When I'm hiding behind
the tree, it means I am completely present behind the tree, but
you can't see me from where you stand. If you take a few steps
to the right or left, you'll see me.

This is the fundamental idea in Kabbalah, that God is right
here all the time. The oneness is right here, but it's hidden. And
so what needs to change? Our angle of vision. Our perception.

Each world gives us, so to speak, a new angle of vision, a
greater perspective, whereby I see more and more of how God
was here all along and how divine oneness embraces and permeates everything and everyone.

According to Kabbalah, we will realize in the future that we
never left the Garden of Eden. In essence, we are still in the
Garden of Eden. We just don't see it. What needs to change is
our way of seeing.

Some people have zoom lenses, and others have wide-angle
lenses. If you are a zoom-lens kind of person, you see all the
details, but you miss out on the greater picture. If you are a
wide-angle person, you see the greater picture but miss the details. The goal in life is to be able to see with both zoom and
wide-angle lenses at the same time, to perceive the most all-
encompassing picture without losing the clarity of detail. It's all
a function of changing the way we see the world and ourselves.

This is the essence of all our challenges and choices. The benefits we enjoy or the consequences we suffer are determined by the choices we make and the attitudes we take. We determine what world we live in by what worldview we adopt. (For more on this, see chapter 4 of my book *Seeing God*.)

So to return to our original question—what's the purpose of the hiddenness?—we can see that hiddenness creates the challenge and the opportunity to strive and grow toward becoming more and more conscious of God's mysterious, all-embracing oneness and experience the joyous ecstasy of love. As the saying goes, "You don't know what you've got till it's gone."

THE WORLDS WE CREATE

Several years ago, I gave my kids Cheerios for breakfast. It said on the front of the Cheerios box that on the back of this box is a three-dimensional Cheerios bumblebee. So I looked at the back of the box and saw a distorted, blurry thing. Have you ever looked at a 3-D book without the goggles? You see a mishmash of misprinted, distorted images. There were no goggles inside the box of Cheerios, but the instructions on the back said to put the picture up to your nose and slowly move it away from your face. Well, I was sitting there waiting for the kids to finish breakfast, so I figured, why not? I put the box up to my nose and slowly moved it away from my face. I didn't get it right. So I put the box up to my nose again, and slowly moved it away. I noticed one of my daughters kicking her sister under the table, like, "Daddy's gone crazy! We knew he was studying Kabbalah or something, but this is crazy. Why doesn't he just eat the Cheerios instead of trying to stuff the box into his nose?"

I wasn't going to give up, however, because it said that there's a three-dimensional bumblebee on the package, and having paid for that box of Cheerios, I wanted to get the full experience. So again I put the Cheerios box up to my nose. I slowly pulled it away, and suddenly I saw it! I shouted, "Oh my gosh!"

My kids jumped up and ran away from the table. Now my kids no longer eat Cheerios. They're afraid it might affect them, too.

The profound lesson on that Cheerios box was that by changing our perceptual focus we can see something that was virtually invisible to us before. The way we see things really determines the way they look.

When Jacob was on his way to Egypt, God said to him, "Jacob, don't worry. Joseph will close your eyes."

The *Zohar* explains that when a person passes away, according to Jewish law, someone has to close the eyes of the deceased. So Jacob was told, in Egypt you're going to pass away, but your beloved son Joseph will be the one to close your eyes.

The *Zohar* asks: Why do we have to close the eyes of the deceased? And the *Zohar* answers: Because the colors, the texture, the shapes of this world are in your eyes; in order to see the next world, someone has to close your eyes.

According to the Kabbalah, we do not see reality as it is. Rather, we see our *perception* of reality, which is the world we live in.

To better understand this, let's borrow some terminology from the philosopher Immanuel Kant. Kant said that there are two aspects to truth: "noumena" are things as they are in themselves, the constituents of reality; "phenomena" are these things as we perceive them. And how we perceive reality can be very different from reality itself.

A familiar example of this discrepancy between reality and our perception is our sense that the world is stationary. Scientists assure us that our planet is whirling around the sun at a speed of 67,000 miles per hour, but my empirical reality testifies that I am totally stationary as I sit here at my computer desk, because the velocity sensors built into human anatomy are limited by gravity.

Similarly, sometimes you meet a person who you feel is worlds apart from you. And she really is: the world that you live in is not the same as the world that she lives in. That's because the way you see reality is very different from the way she sees reality. And the way you see reality actually creates your world. This is what is meant by phenomena.

The worlds of action, formation, and creation are the worlds of phenomena. They reflect reality as it appears to us, with our limited perspective. Noumena, reality as it is, makes up the world of *atzilut*, the world of emanation. As we ascend higher and higher through the three worlds, we get a broader perspective and come closer to discerning more and more what is true about reality but has been hidden.

Atzilut	World of Emanation	Noumena: reality itself
Beriyah	World of Creation	Phenomena: perceptions of reality
Yetzirah	World of Formation	
Asiyyah	World of Action	

As we mentioned earlier, the prophet Zechariah said regarding the messianic age, "In that day, God will be one and His name will be one." Strange. Isn't God already one? This statement is saying that although God is always one, in the present world of phenomena we do not perceive that oneness. God is one, but His "name"—which suggests the way we describe God, based on how we perceive God—is not yet "one." In the time of redemption when our consciousness will evolve to the highest perspective, the highest world, we will actually perceive the oneness of God as it truly is. "God will be one and His name will be one."

For the same reason, when Jews recite, "Hear, O Israel, the Lord is our God, the Lord is One" (Deuteronomy 6:4)—the ultimate affirmation of the oneness of God—we cover our eyes. We realize that we don't see this oneness. But one day we will see this oneness, because our consciousness will evolve to a broader perspective. And the hidden oneness of God will be revealed, and we will finally realize that only love is real.

Our journey in life is all about perspectives. Our goal is to achieve the greatest perspective, which will be the highest world. From that world we will come the closest to seeing everything from the perspective of the source of everything. We will come the closest to getting God's perspective.

That's when the hidden will be found. That's when the oneness and the love will become obvious, and we will bubble over with joy and laughter at the realization of how it was there all the time—only our limited perspectives fooled us and hid this truth.

Piercing through Perspectives

When I was in high school, I got a job as a security guard. I had to wear the standard uniform: a blue cap, a light blue shirt with the emblem "Pinkerton Security Guard" on the upper sleeves, and pants with a stripe down the side. I was wearing my uniform on my way home one day. As I stood at the bus stop, I took off my Pinkerton hat. Of course, underneath it was my *kipah* (skullcap). At that time I had a beautiful *kipah* with white roses and my name embroidered on it. The only other person standing at the bus stop was a young boy. He looked at me and started to chuckle. I didn't know what he was laughing at. I saw that he wanted to say something to me, but he was feeling uncomfortable. Finally he got the courage to say, "'Scuse me, sir, but the lining of your hat stayed on your head."

I said, "I beg your pardon?"

He repeated, "The lining of your hat stayed on your head."

I didn't know what he was talking about. I reached up to my head and felt my *kipah*. "Oh, thank you," I stammered, and put my hat back on.

What to me was obviously a *kipah*, a sign of reverence that

I am always standing in the presence of God, to another person was a detached hat lining, a humorous faux pas worthy of *Candid Camera*. I held myself back from laughing out loud so as not to seem even more weird. But the contrast of our perspectives was funny.

So too, as we pierce through the worlds of perception and uncover more and more of the hidden truth, we will laugh with joy at the humorous contrast between what we thought and what really is. And we will appreciate how the hidden was for the sake of the revelation. The darkness enabled us to see the light.

THE JOURNEY TO PARADISE

Ascending past the worlds of our limited perspectives is the key to understanding one of the great mystical stories of the Talmud.

This famous story tells about four sages who entered *pardes*, which is translated as "orchard" or "paradise." In Kabbalah, *pardes* refers to the highest mystical realms. The four sages were Ben Azzai, Ben Zoma, Alisha ben Abuya, and Rabbi Akiva. Just before they embarked on this inner journey, Rabbi Akiva turned to his fellow travelers and said, "When you get to the place of pure marble, don't say, 'Water, water.'" As a result of this mystical excursion, Ben Azzai died, Ben Zoma went insane, and Alisha ben Abuya became a heretic. Only Rabbi Akiva entered in peace and emerged in peace.

Let's discuss this trip. Where did they go? How does one get there? What is the place of pure marble? What's wrong with saying, "Water, water"? Why does the *pardes* cause one great sage to die, another to go crazy, and another to become a heretic? What did Rabbi Akiva know that enabled him to emerge safely?

One of the greatest Kabbalists ever, the Ari (Rabbi Yitzhak Luria), who lived in the sixteenth century, tells us that these rabbis decided that they would journey to the world of creation through meditation.

As the four rabbis ascended through the worlds, they uncovered more and more of God's oneness. To graphically understand this, look at the following picture:

•　　•　　　　　•　•

What do you see? Four dots, four separate dots. I have a secret for you: they really are not four separate dots, they are two circles. You say, "Rabbi, I'm telling you, I see four separate dots." That's because you are looking at only one dimension of the picture. The other dimensions are hidden. When you see this picture of two circles in one dimension, all you can see is the four dots visible in your one dimension.

But now let's say you can see two dimensions:

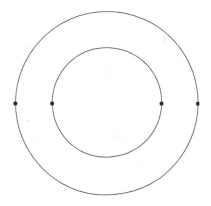

Now you can see that there are indeed two circles, two concentric circles. I have another secret for you: they're not really two circles. I know they look like two circles. That's because you're seeing only two dimensions. If you could see three dimensions, you would see that this is really a picture of a donut (in geometry, a shape known as a torus). The separate dots and circles are really part of one donut, but in one-dimensional or two-dimensional vision you could not see their unity.

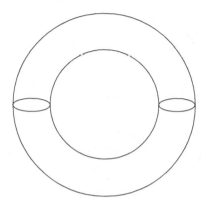

Our minds only perceive three dimensions, but imagine if I were to give you glasses that enabled you to see beyond the third dimension and the fourth dimension. What would that donut look like?

Divine oneness.

But you can't imagine it, any more than a two-dimensional being could imagine a donut. Some scientists are now telling us that there are really twenty-six dimensions to reality (which is interesting because in Hebrew, twenty-six is the numerical equivalent of God's ultimate name, YHVH).

This, then, was goal of the four sages' meditative journey into higher consciousness. They wanted to see beyond the donut. They wanted to see the oneness that includes multiplicity while remaining one. While in this world, they could see only fragmentation and multiplicity. (Seeing from the perspective of the world of action is analogous to seeing only one dimension of the donut.) They wanted to ascend through higher levels of consciousness, so that they would be able to see reality from the highest perspective, as it truly is: one. According to the Ari, the four sages were mystically working their way from the world of action, where we are now, to the world of creation.

What did they specifically want to see? The Ari tells us that they wanted to see what the commandments look like from the perspective of the world of creation. They wanted to see the first set of tablets that Moses brought to us from the top of Mount Sinai.

During the revelation at Sinai, the Jewish people took an incredible leap up the ladder of consciousness into the world of creation. Moses was bringing them the tablets, the Ten Commandments, but they did not look like two slabs of stone, as they later appeared from the perspective of world of action. The Midrash tells us that these tablets were engraved by "the finger of God." The letters went through to the other side, and they read the same on both sides, which of course is logically impossible. This perhaps suggests that the Israelites were able to read them from both the human and divine perspective. Unfortunately, because the Israelites committed the sin of the Golden Calf, they dropped from this lofty perspective and fell back into the lowest level of consciousness. The tablets turned to material substance, heavy stone, and Moses, unable to bear their weight, dropped them. The second tablets, which Moses himself chiseled out of stone, were on the level of the world of action.

Ben Azzai, Ben Zoma, Alisha ben Abuya, and Rabbi Akiva decided they wanted to see the commandments from a perspective closer to the way God sees them. Rabbi Akiva said, "When you get to the place of pure marble, don't say, 'Water, water.'" What's the pure marble? The Ari explains that Rabbi Akiva was giving them a hint to protect them from the dangers of the revelation they were about to have. In Hebrew, *shesh*, the word for marble, also means "six." The first tablets, we are told, were six cubits high (a cubit was about eighteen inches). "The pure six" therefore refers to the pristine tablets. Rabbi Akiva warned them that when they got to the pure six, when they succeeded in seeing the commandments from the perspective of the world of creation, "Don't say 'Water, water.'" In Jewish tradition, the commandments and the lessons behind them are symbolized by water, because of their life-giving properties and because they are accessible only to the humble (as water always flows downward).

So why not say "Water, water"? Because when seen from the perspective of the world of creation, the commandments would look so different from the commandments they knew in the world of action that it was very likely they would say, "Water, water," meaning that there are two different tablets. The way the commandments read in the world of creation and the way they read in the world of action are so different, even contradictory, that one might erroneously conclude that one of the readings is false. This is what Rabbi Akiva was warning his colleagues against.

In the world of creation you realize that there is nothing but God and that you, therefore, have no free choice; the story of life is a monologue all scripted by the Author, and you are just a character playing out His will. However, when you understand the commandments from the perspective of the world of action, then you have free choice to obey or disobey God's commandments—life is a dialogue between God and us. Although God is the Author, mysteriously you contribute to the story.

Of course, in reality, in the world of emanation, the truth goes beyond the either/or of one versus the many, monologue versus dialogue, determinism versus free choice.

What happened? Ben Azzai died. He couldn't come back to this world. Once he saw that there is nothing but God's oneness, he misunderstood that multiplicity and free choice were just an illusion; he therefore concluded that there was no significance to his individual existence on earth.

Ben Zoma went crazy. The paradox was too much for him to handle. He insisted on holding on to his paradigm of either/or—that life is either one or many, determinism or free choice, monologue or dialogue. But the contradiction before him was undeniable, and it drove him crazy.

Alisha ben Abuya became a heretic. He said, "I don't need

to follow the commandments as they appear in the world of action. I see now that I'm beyond it all. There are no borders or boundaries, just divine oneness. And all is predetermined, so whatever I choose to do is exactly what I was destined to do."

Only Rabbi Akiva was able to live with the paradox. Only Rabbi Akiva was able to understand that the whole picture of truth is not captured by the perspective of the world of action, nor the world of formation, nor even by the world of creation. The ultimate truth belongs to the highest perspective of the world of emanation, which is really God's perspective. All these other worlds offer partial perspectives and therefore contradictory understandings. He understood that one and many, determinism and free choice, monologue and dialogue, are all the two sides of the one coin of God's truth. He was willing to accept that God's unlimited reality is beyond the either/or of our limited perceptions.

It's like the famous story about five blind men who wanted to find out what an elephant looks like. One fellow said, "An elephant is long and thin," because he was feeling the tail. Another man said, "No, no! An elephant is like a thick hose," because he was touching the trunk. Another said, "What are you talking about? An elephant is like the trunk of a tree," because he was holding on to the leg. They each had a different, true, albeit partial, experience of an elephant.

What is it that Rabbi Akiva understood? How did he alone emerge from the journey to the *pardes* unscathed?

The Talmud says that Rabbi Akiva entered in peace and emerged in peace. The Talmud is telling us that he emerged in peace *because* he entered in peace. Rabbi Akiva knew the secret of peace.

Shalom, the Hebrew word for peace, really means completeness, wholeness. What is the secret of peace? Peace is not when everybody agrees. Total agreement can never happen, simply because we all have different perspectives of the one reality. The Talmud teaches that, just as each person's face is different from the next person's face, so too do each person's opinions, ideas, and philosophy differ.

Peace is the ability to realize that all the various perspectives are really partial perspectives of a whole picture. The truth is greater than the sum of all those parts. Rabbi Akiva understood that the path to paradise was paradox. He was able to make peace with the apparent conflict.

In addition, as we have seen, Rabbi Akiva was a master of humor. He, like the king's adviser in Rebbe Nachman's story, never took one perspective as the be-all and end-all for understanding the ultimate truth. He was able to laugh his way into paradise and back.

However, each of the other sages was just like the blind man with his arms wrapped around the elephant's leg. Each was absolutely sure that he knew what an elephant is shaped like. And so too the other sages took their perspective too seriously. They were all certain that their view of reality was accurate. And it is. But it is a *partial* accurate view of reality.

We need to know the secret of peace and the art of laughter. Ultimate peace (which really means ultimate completeness) can include two ideas that seem to be contradictory. From a higher perspective, we'll realize they weren't contradictory. They were different perspectives of one complete truth. There were not four separate dots; there was one whole donut. When we will grasp this truth we'll have a good laugh.

In Summary

According to Kabbalah, God has hidden Himself, His oneness, from us so that we can find it, realize it, and experience it. However, since you and I are sparks of God, it is as if God were hiding Himself from an aspect of Himself. Therefore, our journey in search of the One is on behalf of the One and for the sake of the One. Our job is to serve God in His process of self-reflection and knowledge. We have been put in this world of hiddenness to find the Divine with us, to discover that we are souls—sparks of the Divine, act accordingly and thereby reflect God's oneness.

As we elevate ourselves spiritually through the worlds of greater and greater perspective, we will uncover more and more the truth of God's oneness beyond the either/or. We will realize more and more that the many are included within the oneness and permeated by it. And we will experience the ecstasy of love.

This is the journey of our lives. This is the journey God has sent us on. This is our divine mission—to become a living reflection of God, reveal the hidden One, and realize love.

7

Why the Big Secret?

A FEW YEARS AGO I was teaching a class about the mysterious, all-embracing oneness of God and how our mission in life was to reveal that oneness and experience love. There was an elderly woman in the audience who seemed to be very annoyed by what I was teaching. With every new point I made, she seemed to be getting more and more irritated. I could not understand what was going on. Generally when I teach these mystical truths, people get very excited and happy to finally hear a sophisticated and spiritual perspective on God and our divine purpose on earth. They feel relieved that God is not an eternal heavenly bully who just wants to boss them around and make them into His slaves. By the end of the class, this woman was steaming; she leaped toward me and demanded, "How come I have never heard this from a rabbi before?"

I explained to her that there are many rabbis who feel that this approach is too dangerous and should be kept a secret. She said, "If I had heard these ideas earlier on in my life, I would not have been an atheist for the last twenty years. Now what am I going to do?"

Why is the secret life of God kept a secret? I will admit that I too think the ideas in this book can be dangerous, because they can easily be misunderstood. Who are we to even talk about the journey to paradise when three out of four great sages were severely harmed by attempting it?

To answer these questions, I need to explain two approaches to God's oneness—monotheism and panentheism (which is not to be confused with pantheism)—and their implications.

What *do* we mean when we say that God is one?

At age three, my son once asked me, "Daddy, God is one, right?"

"Yes."

"Well, when does He turn two?"

He sure surprised me, and I realized how complicated it would be for me to explain the real meaning of God's oneness to a three-year-old.

Generally, "God is one" is understood to mean that there are no other beings listed under the category of gods—there is just one entry, "God."

When Moses came to the pharaoh of Egypt, conveying the message from God that he should let the Israelites go, the pharaoh said, "Who is this god? I never heard of him."

The Midrash tells us that the pharaoh searched his archives and brought out a list of deities. He proceeded to read: "The god of Moab, the god of Ammon, the god of Zidon . . ." and finally he announced, "See, I have read the entire list, and the name of your god is not in any records."

The pharaoh was a polytheist and believed in a multitude of gods. But from the time of Abraham, who popularized monotheism, the Jewish people believed that there is only one God licensed to practice—the one and only "God." There are no others.

Even when most of the world became convinced of the truth of this view, people continued to believe that there were many other "things" besides God, like tables, chairs, rocks, trees, and so on. There was one God, and then there was the rest of the stuff.

Kabbalah teaches that this is dead wrong. That God is *one* is an absolute statement. It does not mean simply that there is one God; it means that there is *nothing but* God.

We find verses in the Torah such as "Unto you it was shown that you would know that the Lord, He is God. There is none else besides Him" (Deuteronomy 4:35). "Know this day and bring it to your heart that the Lord, He is God in heaven above and the earth beneath; there is none else" (Deuteronomy 4:39). These words are taken very, very seriously.

In general, the tradition that started with Abraham has been described as monotheism. And monotheism means there's one God, there are no other gods. This is understood to mean that God is like a monarch ruling over this world as His kingdom. However, monotheism presents great problems for the human ego.

Basically the message of monotheism is that in the beginning there was God, and He decided for some strange reason to create me. So now there is God, and alongside of Him there is me. And, of course, standing next to God, I feel like nothing. He is infinite and I am infinitesimal. He is eternal and I am temporal. He is Almighty and I am a frail weakling. He is the All-Knowing Spirit and I am a dumb earthling. In short, the more we compare ourselves with God, the worse we feel about our puny selves.

Monotheism creates and nurtures the feeling of a dichotomy between the human and the Divine. We are separate from God, and compared with God we are infinitely smaller than the period at the end of this sentence. If you are a monotheist, then take a good look at that dot and know your true size and worth. This is the message of monotheism: There is one God, and you are not He.

GREEN WITH ENVY

Hidden deep in the psyche of many of us is a jealousy that eats away at our confidence in our stature and significance. It causes us much distress and sadness.

Why does it cause sadness? Whenever you feel sad, it must mean that you had certain expectations that things could be different. If you come for breakfast and all you see is cornflakes, then you're not sad; you had no expectations that it would be any other way. Now imagine if for breakfast you were always served sunny-side-up eggs with a hot cup of coffee and freshly squeezed orange juice, and then one day you walk in and there are just cornflakes; you would be disappointed and saddened because you had had a greater expectation. And if you saw someone else having eggs, you'd feel jealous.

You can't be sad if you can't compare your present situation to one that is better. You can't be sad about something unless you had an expectation that it could have or it should have been some other way. You can't be jealous unless you see that someone else has what you expected for yourself. God has it all, and many of us are feeling jealous of God.

This jealousy, however, is generally subconscious, because most of us are in denial about it. If you admit it, you could find yourself called a heretic. But many of us are jealous of God's infinite happiness, His absolute perfection.

Nietzsche said, "If there were a God, I could not bear not being He." Deep down inside, a lot of us would agree. We ask: "Why can't I be God? Why are You the big God? Why do You sit on your holy throne in heaven? Why do You get to loll around in Your ivory tower, removed, absolved of all the struggles and pains of this world? Let's switch roles for a couple of eons and see how You do in this pit called Earth that You created for us."

This childish feeling of jealousy, if not properly addressed, turns from anger to rage to depression. And finally, we simply have to deny the existence of God to relieve our aching soul. In other words, monotheism, when taken too seriously, leads to atheism. We must get rid of God because we can't stand feeling like nothing next to the Almighty One and Only.

Imagine that you are an artist looking for a roommate. Someone inquires about the extra room and it turns out he too is an artist. Sounds great—you'll have a lot in common. He moves in, and all of a sudden the phone rings like never before.

"Hi, is the artist in?"

You say, "Yeah, this is Jeff speaking."

"No, isn't there an artist there named Harry?"

"Oh, yeah, you mean my new roommate. Harry . . . it's for you!"

The phone rings again. "Hi, I'm looking for Harry, the artist." And this goes on for days. How long would it take before you started feeling challenged, insecure, inferior, and jealous?

If you can't deal with the jealousy of your new roommate—the one and only artist that everyone worships—then what do you do? You evict him. Of course, you would never admit to your jealousy. You come up with all kinds of excuses why he can't continue to live in your apartment. But basically, you just can't take the competition.

In a manner of speaking, it's possible to feel this way about God too. If you feel like nothing next to God, then either you have got to go or He has got to go. When you're in this mindset, in order for you to believe in yourself, you must disbelieve in God.

Atheism can often be a way of self-preservation. My self-esteem is obliterated, my ego is crushed, when I have to believe in the one and only God who is always looking over my shoulder, always judging me, and telling me what to do.

I once saw a comic strip showing a frustrated man complaining, "I am willing to compromise—but God always has to have it His way." To this, a monotheist might add: "And even when I give in and do it His way, it's never good enough. I can never match His greatness, His goodness, and His perfection."

Thinking like this, after a while people get fed up with religion and simply deny the "Big Egomaniac in the Sky." Finally, they can feel better about themselves, or so they think.

However, when they finally muster up the guts to deny the existence of God, they are left with the empty feeling and depressing realization, "If there is no God, then I am just an accident without meaning. I'm coming from nowhere and I'm going nowhere." And there they are back to feeling like the speck of dust they so hoped to avoid.

We can't live with Him and we can't live without Him.

When we reach this dismal dead-end, most of us go into denial and bury this realization. We try to "eat, drink, and be merry" in order to drown the gnawing dissatisfaction inside. As in the old joke, we say: "I've given up looking for the truth—now I'm just looking for a good fantasy." We hope that a vacation in Bali, or a sexy new date, or a bungee-jumping experience will somehow keep the angst from surfacing. But none of those things ever proves the solution to the problem, because in a moment of weakness, the soul's silent scream for meaning and significance becomes deafening.

THE SOLUTION

Kabbalah offers the solution.

It explains that there really is no such God who exists in the one-and-only God category, while we exist in the everything-else category. God *is* the one and only, but not in the way that most people think. Kabbalah reveals the true meaning of divine oneness.

The monotheistic image of God was very essential in the early stages of humanity's development. However, at a certain point in our spiritual evolution, when monotheism was taken to an extreme, it became problematic, and for some people, even counterproductive.

I know that this can sound very confusing, since Judaism is generally understood as a monotheistic religion and its founder,

Abraham, as the first promoter of monotheism. And I am not saying that monotheism is wrong. What I am saying—and what Kabbalah is saying—is that monotheism is not the whole picture.

At a certain stage in the development of civilization, humanity was ready for a new consciousness, and the simple understanding of God provided by monotheism had to go.

In a strange way, atheism helped. It destroyed the childish conceptual graven image of God and thereby paved the way for a higher understanding of God. This understanding of God, as explained by Kabbalah, has been here all along. (In fact, Abraham himself is believed to be the author of one of the foundational kabbalistic texts, the *Sefer Yetzirah*.) However, the world was not ready for that level of abstraction for several thousand years. It had to go through a mental evolution, of which monotheism was an essential cornerstone, before it could see the whole picture. This is why the ancient teachings of Kabbalah have only become popular of late.

Kabbalah tells us that there is no truth to the experience of a separate "me" standing next to God feeling like nothing. Kabbalah reveals that in actuality we exist *within* God.

The reason we don't experience that beautiful mystical truth is because of our distorted perception. The dichotomy that we sense between ourselves and God is in essence a function of the way we think and the way we act (as explained earlier). There really is no separation between the human and the Divine. We are different but not separate. We are in a complete state of oneness with the Divine, within the Divine. It is only the way we think, reinforced by the way we act, that creates a perception and feeling of ourselves as independent and separate from the greatness of God. This is what is meant by the verse in the Book of Isaiah (59:2): "It is only your wrongdoings that separate you from your God."

We are included within the Divine, and with the right attitude and appropriate behavior we can experience this truth. In other words, we already exist within God and are one with God. There is nothing that we can do that would change that. However, if we want to experience that and enjoy that, then it is up to us to think, speak, and act accordingly.

Now, don't get me wrong here. Kabbalah is not saying that you are the Almighty God. As has already been made clear, Kabbalah is saying that you and I are souls, aspects and expressions of the Almighty God.

This is a completely different understanding of the oneness of God.

Monotheism suggests that there is God and there is me. And there is an infinite gap that separates us. But according to Torah and Kabbalah, there is nothing but God and nothing besides God, because everything is within God. Nothing exists apart from the Divine; all is included in the Divine. And here we are, within the Divine. Take a moment to contemplate this wonderful secret. Take a lifetime to live it and celebrate it.

When we embrace Kabbalah's understanding of God, we no longer feel a dichotomy and separation between God and ourselves. There is no competition and no reason for jealousy. Would the heart be jealous of the body? Would any organ of the body feel threatened by the whole body? Of course not.

However, there is a serious distinction between these metaphors and the truth about our relationship with God. If the body were missing a heart, it could not exist. This, however, is not true about God. God can exist without us. God doesn't need us. God freely chose to create us and include us within His mysterious oneness.

This is the ultimate act of love. God freely shares His divine splendor with us all. All we have to do is receive it by knowing this truth and living it. Then we will see—before our very eyes—that everyone is a revelation of Divinity, shining in different colors.

God is one and we are one with God, although we are not the same as God. When you know that you are one with someone, you don't feel threatened and you don't feel jealous. And, of course, there is no competition. You share each other's joy and you share each other's pain.

PANTHEISM VERSUS PANENTHEISM

Do not confuse these ideas with pantheism. Kabbalah is absolutely not pantheistic. Pantheism means that God equals the universe. Therefore, God minus the universe equals nothing. Kabbalah teaches that God minus the universe still equals God. The universe does not add to or detract from the completeness of God.

In addition, pantheism holds that nature is an inevitable expression of God. Kabbalah, by contrast, unequivocally states that God freely created nature. God did not have to create the world—He simply wanted to.

This perspective is generally called panentheism, which means that all is included within the Divine. *Pantheism* derives from *pan,* "all," and *theo,* "god." In other words, all is the Divine. But *panentheism* comes from *pan,* "all," plus *en,* "inside," and *theo,* "god": all is within the Divine.

We could say that panentheism is somewhat of a combination of monotheism and pantheism.

Panentheism agrees with monotheism that there is just one God and we are not God. However, it disagrees with the idea that we have an independent existence and that we are relatively nothing next to God.

Panentheism agrees with pantheism that there's just God, but it disagrees with the notion that we are God.

According to panentheism, there is just God, and we exist within God. And although we do not have an independent existence, we are certainly not nothing. We are not God, but we are godly.

PANENTHEISM

There is only God's oneness; all (universe,
nature, humans, etc.) are included within God.

MONOTHEISM

There is only one God; nature exists apart
from God and is ruled by God.

PANTHEISM

The universe is God; nature embodies God.

POLYTHEISM

There are many gods; different gods rule
different forces of nature.

There can be a down side to the panentheistic approach.
According to monotheism, we at least have an independent identity, although it is relatively infinitesimal next to the one and
only God. According to panentheism, we have no independence
at all. Our sense of independent identity is merely an illusion
based on a perceptual error. Therefore, if we are selfish and care
only about doing what we want rather than what God wants,
we will eventually feel like absolutely nothing. Selfishness is actually self-denial. We are cutting ourselves off from the very
source, ground, context, and content of ourselves—God. Imagine a person in your mind who is only a figment of your imagination. Suppose that imaginary person decides to deny his or her
connection to you and seek a life independent of you. Crazy,
right?

Other than God, there are no self-defined independent beings. All are included within God. You and I are distinct and
other than God, but nonetheless absolutely one with God. There
is a distinction between the human and the Divine, but no dichotomy or separation. There is just a mysterious oneness that
includes multiplicity and otherness while remaining one. When
we choose to acknowledge this and do God's will, we discover

that there is just God's oneness, and we experience the ecstasy of ultimate love.

When two people truly love each other, they experience a oneness that encompasses their unique individualities. I'm not you and you're not me, yet we are one. The equation of love is $1 + 1 = 1$. The mystery and ecstasy of love are a taste of panentheism—the true meaning of God's absolute oneness.

From a monotheistic point of view, we feel separate and far from God. From a panentheistic point of view, we are one with God and can never get far. If we do feel far, then we are creating the distance only in our minds. We feel distant because we have adopted the wrong mind-set and behaved accordingly. When we do so, we will feel like absolutely nothing.

However, if we realize we are one with God and think and act accordingly, then we experience sharing in His glory, His greatness, and His vitality. Then we taste the sweetness of sharing timelessness because we discover the true divine source, ground, context, and content of our lives. Even though we are not God, we are so much one with God that we stop feeling like insignificant weaklings and start enjoying the greatness of God that we share.

THE ULTIMATE SELF

According to Kabbalah, the real work you have to do in your life is to overcome your egotistical illusions about being separate, independent, and self-defined. You've got to realize that independent of God, you're absolutely nothing. Independent of the divine all-encompassing reality, you're absolutely nothing.

For most people, that is really frightening. But when you let go of your ego, you discover an even greater sense of self at one with God. In this state of ecstasy you experience that there's nothing but God. And yet you do not, in any way, have any fantasies that you are God. When you know God at this level, then you are deeply self-aware, but not self-conscious.

I have a personal example of such a moment of awareness. I was once performing a concert of original music that I had composed. When I first got out on stage, I felt there was me, (independent reality stuck in its ego shell) and there was the audience. I had to please them, and they had to approve of me. There was tension in the air, and I was feeling really self-conscious and feared that I was going to blow it.

The curtains opened, there was this crowd of people looking at me, and suddenly I totally forget my song. I don't read music, so whenever I do a concert it is always by memory. At this moment, I had lost my memory. I was totally petrified—what was I to do? At that moment, I realized, I would have to totally surrender my ego, let go, and trust God. With perfect faith, I put my fingers on the keyboard, and the miracle happened. My fingers went exactly to the right notes and gracefully danced across the keys playing a song. I suddenly experienced myself as the instrument of God. God was playing through me. All I had to do was get my ego out of the way.

Unfortunately, I did not quite succeed. Suddenly I was overcome by self-consciousness again. I heard the voice of my ego start to speak: "Hey, David, you're doing really well, you're doing really well." And that's exactly when I messed up; I made a big mistake and started playing the wrong notes. Fumbling in embarrassment and growing more desperate by the second, I threw my ego off the stage, let go again, and found myself back in tune.

The annihilation of self-consciousness is a joyous and liberating experience. This is what happens to you when you live panentheism. You don't think you are God, but you do experience yourself as an instrument of God. You feel filled with godliness, but your ego does not proclaim itself to be God. You realize that there is nothing but God, because you have no independent existence—your distinct identity as other than God is mysteriously included within God. In that moment you experience the miracle of timeless and endless love.

THE BODY'S MESSAGE

What is it that keeps suggesting that I do have an independent reality?

My body.

The body suggests that the real "I," my true self, lives in this sack of skin.

The first man and woman didn't have bodies of skin; they had bodies of light. In the Garden of Eden there were no shadows. Shadows are produced by something interfering with the rays of light. An object blocks the light because it has an independent reality that interferes with the light. In the Garden of Eden, there were no shadows. There were distinct entities, but the light permeated everything without obliterating these distinctions.

It was only after Adam and Eve ate of the Tree of Knowledge of Good and Bad that shadows appeared, and Adam and Eve began to experience themselves confined within bodies of skin that separated them from the rest of reality, God.

Before their transgression, they were one with that reality, but the choice to eat of the forbidden fruit changed their perception of what is truly real. After the transgression, consciousness dropped into the world of action—the very lowest level of perception—where the oneness of God is most concealed.

Now our job is to climb the ladder of consciousness and reveal the hidden oneness of God that actually continues to permeate and embrace everything.

In the lowest world, where God's oneness is most concealed, we perceive God's oneness in a monotheistic way: there's me, there's God, and we are separate. But as we move up the ladder of the worlds, we discover that that infinite gap between us starts to melt away. When we reach the perception of the highest worlds, all the illusions of separate reality disappear. In the highest state of consciousness we experience the true meaning of God's all-inclusive oneness and discover that only love is real.

This further explains the meaning of the journey of the four sages who went to *pardes*. The place of departure for their meditative, metaphysical journey was the lowest world, where God's oneness is perceived through the eyes of monotheism. Their destination was a higher world, where oneness is seen through the eyes of panentheism.

Ben Zoma couldn't deal with the apparent contradiction between having and not having an independent reality. He went mad trying to put together the perspective of God from the lower world and the perspective of God from the higher world.

Ben Azzai died because he felt so drawn to the oneness that he refused to return to his body in the lower world of separation.

Alisha ben Abuya became a heretic because he concluded that all borders and boundaries are simply illusions. There is nothing but God, and there is no other. He became a pantheist, believing that all is God, including himself. This is why, in protest against his self-delusion, people began to call him Acher, which means "the other one." They wanted to remind him that he is other than God. Acher couldn't hear it and began to do all sorts of things forbidden by Jewish law. He believed that he was beyond all limits. He was now an enlightened being who knew the truth about the real world—that laws and boundaries are merely illusions.

This is the danger of panentheism. People like Acher may misunderstand panentheism and confuse it with pantheism. This is why it is essential to first teach people monotheism, even though it has some problematic side effects. It must be well engraved into the mind and hearts of human beings that they are *not* God. People must first believe that they are other than God, even if they will mistakenly think that they are separate from God and comparatively insignificant. Nonetheless, it is critical for their spiritual development to think this way so that when panentheism is finally introduced to them, they will not think they are God. They will be ready to understand that all is included within God.

Monotheism is the prerequisite to panentheism. Monotheism prepares us for the ultimate truth of panentheism. If you are introduced to panentheism prematurely, before your sense of independent self is evolved (even though it is an illusion), then you might think that you do not even have a distinct self other than God—that all is God—and that borders are simply an illusion.

There is timing to education. You cannot teach children the whole truth and nothing but the truth right away. Sometimes you have to conceal the whole truth and only reveal part of the truth, even though there will be misunderstandings and derivative negative side effects. Nonetheless, in the long run it will be worth it.

Reward and punishment is an essential principle to instill within children to guide their behavior. However, at a certain point in their development, you will have to teach them to do the right thing because it is right and not because of promise of reward or fear of punishment. When children are in grade one or two, you create for them a good-deeds chart and give them points so that they can accumulate enough points to get a prize. However, once they get to grade three, you have to begin to introduce them to a higher motivation for their behavior. Otherwise, points begin to stifle the children's development toward having the right attitude about why they do what they do. So, too, monotheism was positive for human development, but at a certain stage it became counterproductive. The time had come for panentheism.

HOLY MISCONCEPTIONS

This is the evolving story of religious beliefs. First humanity needed to believe that there is only one God and that we are not God. We needed to believe that our separate and independent existence is real. Otherwise, we would have never developed a sense of self and learned to value borders and boundaries. We also needed to understand that next to God we are relatively small so that we would fear God and control our hunger for power. Although the fear of God is not an ideal way to motivate a person, and many of us resist it and find the concept a turn-off, it can sometimes be a necessary tool. The goal is to reach God through love and awe, which are inspired by panentheism.

However, at a certain stage of human development, mono-theism stifled our healthy progress and caused us to lose all self-esteem. At this point atheism became a natural reaction; it helped us recover some of our self-respect and free ourselves from our overwhelming fear of God. But the image of God pre-sented by monotheism was only partial and therefore mislead-ing. Now we are ready for the higher perception of panentheism. When we begin to lose our self-respect and rebel against God, then the full truth of panentheism as expressed in Kabbalah must be revealed. We can now at last get in on the big secret.

It was all a matter of time.

Both panentheism and monotheism can have positive and negative effects upon humanity. Each approach is positive when it comes at the right time, and it is negative when it's at the wrong time. The monotheistic approach is positive when that's the way I need to see things. And it is negative when it continues to be the perspective of religion even though I am ready to un-derstand reality from a higher perspective of panentheism.

The Dialect

This was the tension between the Hasidim and the Mitnagdim. In Jewish history there was a very furious conflict between these two movements. The Hasidic movement was founded by the Baal Shem Tov in the eighteenth century in Eastern Europe and continues to be a huge movement today. The Vilna Gaon led the Mitnagdim.

Some explain that the tension was over the educational question of whether ordinary people were ready for the higher perspective of panentheism. The Hasidim believed the time had come to teach the masses the secret of God's true oneness as expressed in Kabbalah. The Mitnagdim, however, felt that such a revelation to the masses was premature and dangerous. They feared that people would fail to understand the real meaning and would confuse panentheism with pantheism, erroneously thinking that everything is God. People would then deny the significance of the commandments, whose very basis is the respect for boundaries and borders. Therefore, introducing the secrets of Kabbalah at this stage of human development would be destructive.

The Hasidim argued the opposite. They contended that if we continued to hide the full truth and keep pushing monotheism, people were going to lose faith. Monotheism had become a turn-off. People couldn't handle the dichotomy between the human and the Divine anymore. The implicit message of human insignificance was now counterproductive and was causing people to choose atheism.

Even though this debate took place in the eighteenth century, I still feel this very dilemma as I write this book. You can be sure that there are some people who are against me for writing it. They will argue that I should first teach people to fear God and put them in their place. However, although I do think that these ideas could be misinterpreted, I believe the time has come to really put people in their place—people have to know that their place is within God.

I have met some people who have a tremendous drive to learn mysticism, but they don't have their feet firmly enough on the ground nor a proper reverence for God. For such people these ideas are dangerous. They will use them for self-aggrandizement and think they are free to do as they please, like Acher. However, I have met more people who are very ready for these ideas and are in spiritual danger if they do not discover them soon.

One of the great Hasidic masters wrote a letter to his followers in which he explained, "We Hasidim fail to appreciate how much we owe our opponents. They were right. The fire of the mystical teachings of Hasidism would have burnt up all of Jewish law. We must be thankful for their opposition. They provided the essential counterbalancing force that kept us in line."

History eventually balances itself out. The left balances out the right, and the right balances out the left. Monotheists balance out panentheists and protect them from becoming pantheists. And panentheists balance out the monotheists so that they don't end up being atheists from a lack of self-esteem.

THE CLOSET BELIEVERS

Now, I have to admit that experientially panentheism is like a psychedelic trip. All in the One and One in the all is a real mind-blowing experience. Therefore, it is necessary to understand that you must hold fast to monotheism in order to experience panentheism. Otherwise the bright light of panentheism could obliterate all the details in life—all the boundaries and the borders—and you end up seeing life through the distorted perspective of pantheism.

This is one of the spiritual dangers of the drug culture. Drug abuse can sometimes be motivated by a yearning to experience the oneness of God. But the psychedelic traveler is trying to jump back into some primordial undifferentiated reality in order to escape the challenges and responsibilities of this world. Kabbalah warns us that there is no such undifferentiated reality. God's oneness includes all the distinctions, diversity, and multiplicity while being absolutely one.

There are very few individuals like Rabbi Akiva who can enter paradise in peace and return to this world in peace. Most people cannot live in both worlds simultaneously. Most people, after they have tasted the ecstasy of the higher perspective of oneness, cannot come back to this world. Most of us cannot live in this practical world filled with details while soaring in the world of oneness. Therefore, we must be monotheists in our daily public life but closet panentheists in our private time. "Six days you shall do your work, but on the seventh day you must rest" (Exodus 23:12).

This is the one of the messages in the story of the tainted grain by the Hasidic master Rebbe Nachman of Breslov:

There was once a king who, along with his friend, observed that the whole kingdom went insane after eating a certain grain. Everyone who went insane began to think they were normal and that it was the king and his friend who were the crazy ones. (Imagine if everybody thought they were frogs and you didn't think you were a frog; you would be considered the nut case in this world.) The king and his friend decided that they too should eat the hallucinogenic grain and join everyone. However, they decided to put a sign on their foreheads so that they would later remember that they had gone insane. This way, although the whole kingdom would be crazy, at least the king and his friend could *know* they were crazy whenever they looked at each other.

This story teaches that we need reminders so that we don't forget that we are bound to God. We live in a crazy world where we believe that we are separate from each other and from God. Only those of us who can put a mark on our foreheads to remind us that we were once "sane," that we once saw the world very differently, can keep a connection with what's real. This is why there is a Jewish tradition to wrap leather straps containing the credo of God's oneness—"Hear, O Israel, the Lord is our God, the Lord is One"—on the arm and forehead, as a reminder that man is bound up with God.

We live in a world where most people think they are separate and that they are normal. Those of us who know better end up pretending that the others are right. However, we need to create reminders that we are just pretending.

So I am sorry to tell you that you can't walk away from this chapter and tell everyone that you are now a panentheist. You have to pretend that you are a monotheist. But when we pass each other on the street, we will wink and acknowledge the oneness that holds us all together. This is the only way that we can live in this practical world.

The Way of Oneness

With this in mind, let us now examine the way monotheism views God's commandments and how differently panentheism would understand them.

According to monotheism, the Almighty God who dwells in the heavenly realms has commanded me to do His will. He can punish me or reward me based on my willingness to comply and act in obedience. Of course, I could decide not to act according to His bidding because I am independent—I have my own mind and will. However, I acknowledge that God is more powerful than I. I would be pretty stupid to pick a fight and try to stand my ground. Why suffer the consequences and bear His wrath? I fear the pain of punishment and the loss of potential reward. Therefore, although this is not what I want to do, I must surrender and obey if I want to survive. Hopefully, in the long run my self-sacrifice will pay off with some big reward. Essentially, monotheism is a religion of fear.

Now let's take a look at the panentheistic way of seeing God and His commandments. From this perspective it is not me against God, but me within God. There is no conflict of interest because I realize that I don't have an independent existence, will, or mind—my true will is an expression of God's will, and my true self is a spark of God. Therefore, to be true to myself and experience oneness with God, I *want* to fulfill the commandments. This is not an act of obedience but really a profound act of self-expression. I understand that if I had God's perspective, then this is what I would really want to do.

It is like when I was toilet-training my son. In the beginning he thought I was nuts. I could see in his eyes that he was thinking, "Daddy, you have got to be kidding. Do you actually want me to give up my freedom of expression and spontaneity and put it into that pot? I just want to let it go whenever and wherever it happens. I am a natural, healthy, and spontaneous kid. It's you adults who are stiff, dogmatic, and uncreative."

Therefore, I created a system of rewards to encourage him to obey me and give up his freedom. Every time he used the pot, he would get a piece of chocolate. However, once he finally got the knack for it, he realized that he did not need a reward as compensation for his self-sacrifice and obedience. He now realizes that this is the more cultured way to behave, and it is what he really wants to do. He no longer feels that he has to obey me; instead, he chooses this behavior as a way to be true to himself as a cultured and sophisticated human being.

This is also true about the commandments of God. In the beginning it seems as if it is God's will against ours. There is conflict, and we must surrender. However, as we evolve, we realize that we do not have an independent will and that our true will is a part of God's. Then we understand that the reward of the commandment is the opportunity to be who each of us is—an expression of God. With this perspective in mind, we fulfill the commandments because we want to and not because we have to. However, if we think that there is a conflict of interest and feel that we are sacrificing our freedom, then we are laboring under an illusion that we are separate and independent of God. (This further explains the Midrash that we mentioned earlier regarding the dispute over how we will relate to the commandments in the future—we won't have to obey them, because it will be clear to us that this is the natural way to behave.)

Thus, for the monotheist, following the commandments is an act of obedience, motivated by fear. But for the panentheist, it is an act of self-expression motivated by love.

When you love somebody, you feel one with that person. If he or she asked you to do something, what would be your response? Would you say, "Who are you to impose yourself on me? I know what you're trying to do; you're trying to make me into your little slave." If you really love someone and know that together you are one, then you would say, "How could I not do it? We're one." There's no competition. There's just oneness.

In the Garden of Eden the snake presented to Adam and Eve

a monotheistic understanding of God. He said, "Do you know the real reason God commanded you not to eat of the Tree of Knowledge? It's because He knows that when you eat it, you too will become as powerful as He. He doesn't want you to evolve too much. Therefore, in order to stifle your growth, He's forbidden it so that He can keep you under His cosmic thumb. He can't afford to let you challenge His omnipotence and possibly usurp His throne."

This is really the problem with the monotheistic understanding of God. It suggests that there is conflict and competition between us and God, that the commandments are meant to get us to surrender our freedom and make ourselves subordinate to God.

When Adam and Eve bought into this attitude, they become mortal. This is because they cut themselves off from the oneness of God and severed their connection to the source and ground of their lives. They began to experience themselves as having bodies of skin, which fed the illusion that they were separate from the rest of reality—God. After they ate of the forbidden fruit they feared death. However, Kabbalah teaches us that death is really an illusion.

When we will leave our bodies in death, we actually return to the higher awareness of our oneness with God. Now, don't misunderstand this. Kabbalah is not encouraging us to commit suicide. It is trying to get us to see that the sense of independence and separateness that the presence of the body suggests is an illusion. We are distinct and other than God, but we are not separate.

When we realize the true meaning of God's oneness, then we transcend death and discover our immortality. We experience that we always interfaced with the immortal God. The more we consciously identify with God, the more we realize we were always one with God. There never was a separation. It was only in our minds. It was only a matter of our perception, knowledge, and behavior.

THE FATE OF CHOICE

We can now reach a deeper understanding of how free choice interfaces with determinism. According to Kabbalah, we and all our choices exist within the context of God's oneness, will, and plan. In other words, we have free choice and yet whatever we choose mysteriously fits into God's plan and fulfills God's all-encompassing will.

This means that we can choose to do other than God's will and yet we cannot oppose God's will. Whatever we choose to do actually serves God. Whether we choose to do evil or choose to do good, our choices will accomplish God's will.

This mystery is well suggested by the artist M. C. Escher in some of his brilliant drawings. In one picture Escher creates a water mill whose waters flow away from the mill and yet end up back at the top of the mill, continuing to propel it. He has another drawing showing a line of men descending a staircase, and yet as we follow them along their way down, they gradually appear to be climbing and mysteriously end up at the top of the stairs.

Indeed, life is like an Escher drawing. Yes, you can do other than God's will—but why would you want to do that? You can go down the stairs, but you will end up climbing them whether you want to or not.

This is what happens in the Purim story. Haman, the wicked minister of the king of Persia, decides to kill the entire Jewish people. However, without any apparent intervention from God, he actually ends up digging his own grave. This same pattern is visible in the story of the Jewish people during their slavery in Egypt. Pharaoh's astrologers tell him that the redeemer of the Jews will soon be born, but he will be defeated by water. Pharaoh therefore decided to have all the newborn Jewish boys thrown into the Nile. Ironically, Moses's mother hides him in a watertight basket and floats it among some rushes by the shore of the Nile. Pharaoh's daughter happens to come to bathe in that very spot and discovers this charming baby. She brings him home to daddy Pharaoh, and they raise him in the palace with a royal upbringing befitting a leader who is destined to free the enslaved Jews from Egypt.

Although Pharaoh chose to oppose God's plan, he actually contributed to its fulfillment. (Again, we can see how dangerous such ideas can be.)

What, then, is the meaning of our choices? Our choices make a difference to us. We determine whether we will experience our love for and oneness with God or whether we will experience ourselves as separate and in conflict.

This brings us back to the verse of Isaiah, "It is only your wrongdoings that separate you from your God." From God's perspective we are never separate from God, but from our perspective, because of the wrong choices that we make, we experience ourselves as separate from Him.

We're often afraid of God's punishment. But what we don't realize is that God doesn't have to punish us. We are already doing a good enough job at it ourselves. The alienation from God that we create through our choices becomes our own hell.

However, when we choose to accord our will with God's will, we create our own heaven—the ecstatic experience of God's oneness and love.

FORGIVENESS IS DIVINE

Despite our best intentions to create our own heaven, there are bound to be a few times when we make mistakes, some of which could have profound consequences and be very discouraging. We might even wonder if we can ever really make it, and whether we will be forever scarred by our past wrongdoings. Will our past hell continue to haunt us?

If I stole something, I can return it. But if I killed somebody, I can't bring that person back to life. While few of us have done anything as seriously wrong as that, we all have in our repertoire many wrongs that we have committed that cannot be undone.

The Talmud tells us, however, that in the future we will see the whole picture and will understand that even our worst wrongdoings, which were surely other than God's will, nonetheless served the completion of the picture in some way.

This is the transformational power of the special day called Yom Kippur, the day of atonement and forgiveness. There is a cryptic verse in the Book of Psalms (139:16) that, the sages say, refers to Yom Kippur: "The days were formed, and one of them is His."

Every day of the year we see the world from our perspective, but there is one day—God's day—when we get a glimpse of the way the world looks from His perspective. This is actually the perspective of the World to Come (the time in history after the messianic age) where you get the whole picture. When we will look back and see the whole picture, we will realize that every act and event contributed to God's plan to actualize ultimate goodness.

Yom Kippur is an amazing day of transformation when our darkest moments from the past turn into light. This is because the light of the World to Come is shining into our world this day.

This is another manifestation of the mysterious relationship between free choice and determinism. On one hand we have free choice to do other than God's will, and yet God is always in control. Although we can do other than God's will, we cannot oppose His will nor undermine His plan. Therefore, when we have done wrong and are sorry for it, we must realize that no matter what we have done, it all fits into God's plan and contributes to the ultimate good.

Here once again we see the danger in the panentheistic approach and understand why it's a big secret. People might interpret this to mean that they can just go ahead and do wrong. They may reason, "What difference does it make, if whatever I do fulfills the will of God?"

We must be reminded that although what we do fulfills God's will, the very choice to go against God separates us from

God. This distance causes us feelings of alienation and spiritual anguish that may even manifest as physical ailment and disease.

It is important to remember that if we sincerely regret our wrongdoings and resolve never to repeat them, our past can be forgiven, recycled, and put toward future good. We can achieve atonement and once again feel at-one-ment with God. When this happens, we experience something even more amazing than God's forgiveness: we actually forgive ourselves.

As mentioned earlier, the Talmud goes so far as to say that if our deep remorse comes from love for God, then our spiritual debts are converted into merit points. In other words, you can even cash in on your wrongdoings by using them as a motivation to come closer to God.

Have you ever fought with someone you loved and then realized how wrong and foolish you were? When you made up, didn't you suddenly feel closer to that person than you did before the fight? You may have even thought, "Maybe we should plan an argument once a month to renew our love." This, of course, is not necessary because there will be plenty of opportunities for problems without having to plan them. The same is true with us and God.

There is a basic rule about rectifying the past: acknowledge that what you did was wrong, regret making that choice, resolve never to do it again, and fix whatever damages you caused. Whatever you cannot fix, let go of it and remember that God is, was, and always will be in control. If you can't fix it, even though you have tried your utmost, don't worry; it too somehow fits into the divine plan and is all for the best.

This idea can be easily misunderstood and abused. We must not think this way before we make choices. We can't say, "Well, if it is meant to be, then it doesn't matter what I choose." It does matter. The difference is between the heaven and hell that you create for yourself and others. The difference is between living in a dark, painful, fragmented world or living in the light and joy of God's oneness and love.

In Summary

The reason for the secretiveness about the secret life of God is that if you knew it before you were ready to know it, you might come to think you were one with God and the same as God. This was the grave mistake of Acher: in the ecstasy of experiencing God's oneness and his oneness with God, he lost touch with the distinctions between human and Divine.

This is a common mistake of two people in love. In the euphoria of their passion, they may lose the healthy sense of how different they are from each other. They may then make some very wrong assumptions, each one thinking, "We are one, so surely what I want is also the only desire of my beloved." Then come the surprises and disappointments and fights.

The Talmud cautions us that love damages borders.

This is why we need monotheism, because even though it promotes feelings of separateness from God and evokes fear of God, it helps us maintain the necessary distinctions. Keeping those distinctions intact allows us to safely enter and exit the paradise of panentheism (where we experience God's all-encompassing oneness), without falling into the destructive trap of pantheism (where all borders between ourselves and God are obliterated).

8

To Know and to Be Known

ONCE WE ARE CLUED into the mysterious truth about the secret life of God, how can we use this powerful knowledge to lead us to a direct encounter with God?

When we search for God, we face two inherent obstacles. The first is the language we use to describe what we know, and the second is the very process of knowing.

In general we describe things in terms of time, space, and comparison to other objects. For example, you could describe this book in terms of time and space as now and here. You could describe it relative to other objects as smaller than your body but bigger than your hand. If you are describing a person, then you could say that George lived for eighty years and died two years ago. He lived in a town ten miles away from here. He was more intelligent than the average person, but he was also less emotional than most people. We have described George in terms of time, space, and comparison to other people.

But these terms cannot be applied when we want to describe and know God. God is the Creator of time, space, and all beings. He therefore transcends these categories. As I explained in chapter 5, although it is common to say that God is "eternal" and "infinite," these terms are incorrect. For most people, "eternal" means something that goes on and on in time. But God is the source of time. Time cannot confine or define God. "Infinite" means something that has no end and goes on and on in space. But God is the source of space. Space cannot confine or define God.

Because descriptive language is inherently relative, it can never be accurate when applied to God. If I describe a table as large or small, it is in relationship to other tables. If I describe it as "a mahogany table," the listener's mind automatically calls up its file image of wood, learned from contrasting mahogany with pine or oak, and so forth. God, however, is the source and creator of everything and therefore cannot be compared to *anything*. Even the core principle of Torah and Kabbalah that God is one is followed by the qualification that this does not mean "one" compared to "two." Therefore, all terminology when applied to God is actually a form of linguistic and conceptual idolatry.

Since people are accustomed to thinking in terms of time, space, and comparisons, they automatically conceive of God as the one and only Almighty being, who has no body, who is eternal in time, and who is infinite in space. This image is not only wrong, it is downright destructive. It is this kind of thinking that contributes to the separation and conflict between humanity and God. It contributes to the mistaken thinking that if God is infinite and I am finite, then we are opposites and mutually exclusive; if God is eternal and I am temporary, than we are opposites and mutually exclusive; if God is one and we are multiple, than we are opposites and mutually exclusive.

This is why (as I explained earlier) it would be more correct to say that God is spaceless, timeless, and nondual. The spaceless can encompass space and be within it and beyond it simultaneously. The timeless can embrace time and be within it and beyond it at the same time. The nondual is not like the number one that is the opposite of two, three, and many. Nonduality is the oneness *before* the number one. It is a oneness that can include the many and fill the many while remaining one. The nondual is the one that can include the many, whereby the many are in the one and the one is in the many. God is totally unique and cannot be compared to any other beings, as the Israelites sang after they crossed the Red Sea:

> *Who is like You among the heavenly powers, O God!*
> *Who is like You, mighty in holiness, too awesome for*
> *praise, doing wonders?* (Exodus 15:11)

In that moment they were struck by the limitations of the relative descriptions of language. The normative terminology we use to describe anything breaks down when it comes to knowing God. Nonetheless, we still talk about God as an almighty eternal and infinite being. This is a little bit crazy, but what can we do? We are stuck; we have no other language available.

Indeed, the Torah is filled with all kinds of puzzling descriptions like "the hand of God," "the back of God," "the face of God," and "the eye of God." These terms would constitute idolatry if the Jewish tradition didn't caution at every step that such metaphors are meant to be taken poetically and not literally, and that we use them precisely because we have no other language for describing God. The Torah sets out to communicate incredibly deep, abstract ideas and must do it in the common language of human beings. However, we must always seek to translate the metaphor into the true experience it was meant to convey.

As long as we remember that these terms are poetic metaphors, they will be useful to direct and focus our minds. But if we forget and take these words literally as describing some eternal infinite all-powerful being "out there," then our spiritual search is doomed to fail.

LOOKING IN ALL THE WRONG PLACES

There are two main reasons why people often fail to find God. The first is that they are looking for the wrong God—a linguistic concept, an idol. They want to capture God with their categorizing minds in neat terms of time, space, and being. This is like trying to catch water with a net.

As a rabbi, I am in the painful position of having to talk about God, who cannot be talked about. We should feel uncomfortable when talking about God, although it is certainly better than talking about our latest acquisitions or gossiping about other people.

When reading the Bible, you should feel uncomfortable with the imagery of the hand of God, the eyes of God, God's anger, and the like. If you feel comfortable with such imagery, then you've missed the whole point, because the Bible is speaking in holy poetry when it refers to God. Ironically, many people take exactly the wrong approach. They think that the Bible is being literal when referring to God and metaphorical when recounting the stories of human beings. On the contrary, the Bible is being literal in its accounts of human beings (although there are also deeper levels of meaning in every story) but poetic whenever it mentions God.

If you read Carl Sandburg's poem that says, "The fog comes in on little cat feet," you do not think that the fog has little feet. Rather, you feel the experience of the poet in the words. Through that metaphor the poet wants to guide you into his experience, which is beyond words. Similarly, when the Jewish tradition refers to God as a father, or lover, or king, it wants to draw us into an experience of that relationship. All references to God in the Jewish tradition are poetic rather than literal.

The other obstacle to knowing God is the limitation inherent in the very process of knowing. When I attempt to know anything, I am the subject and the thing that I seek to know is the object. In addition, there must be some degree of distance and separation between the subject and the object. Your eye can see almost everything, but it cannot see itself. "Knowing" implies two separate entities: the knower and the known.

However, you cannot know God in this normative way, because God is the source of all knowing. God is the source of all consciousness. Your very ability to think comes from God, who is the source of all thinking. How can you think about the source of all thinking? How can your mind hope to comprehend the source and ground of all minds?

Yet if you want to know God, then you must seek the source of all knowing. You must search for the source of all searching.

This is why we cannot come to actually know God by philosophical inquiry. The philosopher tries to make God into an object of his mind. He thinks that he is the subject and that he can understand God as the object of his inquiry. Even if the philosopher comes up with a brilliant thesis about God, he has gained an idea, but he has lost God. God is not an idea. God is the source of all ideas.

In general, you are the knowing subject and everything else is the object to be known. But with God the relationship is just the opposite. God is the subject and you are the object. God is the knower and you are the known.

In truth, God is like the thinker, and the entire universe is His thought. According to the Kabbalah, creation is an act of divine thought. We come into existence through God's thinking of us, so to speak. We exist only as long as God continues to think of us. If at any point God forgot us, poof! We would have no existence.

This is a crucial idea. If I create a table, I can walk away from it, and the table will continue to exist. But if I create a table in my mind, it will exist only as long as I continue to think of it. At the moment I stop thinking of the table, it is gone. That is what Torah means when it says that God creates the universe anew in every moment. Without the constant process of divine thought, the universe, which is a divine thought-form, could not exist into the next moment.

The great eighteenth-century Hasidic master and author of the *Tanya,* Rabbi Shneur Zalman of Liadi, teaches:

> The Holy One knows all the created beings, and His knowledge of them adds neither plurality nor novelty to Him. For He knows everything by knowing Himself. . . . The Holy One actually embraces each and every creature with His thought and His knowledge of all the created beings. For His knowledge is indeed its life force and that which brings it into existence.

You and I are made of thought—of consciousness. Kabbalah teaches that the more conscious we are, the more real we are, the more alive we are, and the more connected we are to the source of consciousness. The less conscious we are, the less alive we are.

That is also what the Oral Tradition means when it says that the holy man is alive even when he dies, and the evil man is dead even while he still alive. Evil people have forfeited the very substance of life, which is consciousness of oneness—consciousness of God. The more we participate in divine consciousness, the more we participate in the very essence of life. We know God the way we know ourselves—not as an object we observe and study, but through direct involvement and participation.

Earlier we discussed the idea of a character existing in the mind of the author. Now take a moment and create in your mind a woman. Don't think of someone that you know. Rather, create a totally new character. Where does that woman exist? In your mind. Therefore, you are the knowing subject and she is the known object. Now imagine this woman in your mind trying to find her creator—you. How is she going to do that? How would this woman who is the object of your mind make you the object of her mind? How could she possibly understand you?

This is the same problem we have in our search for God.

Relative to anything that we seek to understand, we are the knower and it is the known. But when we turn our thoughts to God, He is the knower and we are the known. He is the subject and we are the object.

Each one of us is like a drop in the ocean trying to comprehend the ocean.

Imagine a sphere encircling you. If this sphere were to represent God, you would describe yourself as being encompassed by this embracing reality that is God. From your perspective, what would you see? You and God. From God's perspective, what does God see? Just God.

From the perspective of the woman you have created in your mind, there is her and you. From your perspective, there's just you.

When something painful happens to you, you may find yourself accusing God: "How could You do this to me?" But from God's perspective, there is just God. No perpetrator and victim. Just God. From that perspective, your accusation appears as ludicrous as your stubbed toe shouting at you, "What are you doing to me?"

In the Book of Isaiah, God exclaims, "My thoughts are not like your thoughts." This means that God's perspective is totally different from our human perspective. Just as a theoretical being who lives in a two-dimensional reality cannot possibly conceive of the perspective of three-dimensional beings such as ourselves, so we cannot possibly conceive of God's perspective.

This essentially is God's answer to Job. Job suffers a series of tragedies: the death of all his children, illness, and material loss. He tries to fathom why God has done this to him, given that he is a good person who has only done good. His friends and his wife offer various perspectives, all of which Job rejects as lacking the ring of truth. Finally God speaks to Job: "Where were you when I laid the foundations of the earth? Declare, if you have understanding. Who determined its measurements, if you know?" God is telling Job that he simply does not have the cosmic perspective to understand what happens in this world.

Job is left with not knowing the answer to human suffering, not because God refuses to tell him, but because there is no way a human being can understand reality from God's perspective, which is ultimate truth.

The sages say that when we get to the next world, we are going to look back at all of human history and see everything as perfect. Even the worst periods of history are going to look wonderful. This means that in that future world, without the limitations of time and space, we will see everything from God's perspective. But now, ensconced as we are in this world of time and space, that perception is simply inaccessible to us. Human beings trying to fathom the divine plan are like someone trying to run Windows 2000 on a 286 computer. We simply do not have the hardware to understand God, who is the ultimate all-inclusive reality.

Now we can appreciate the complications in seeking to understand and know God. The rules of normative knowing simply do not apply here. God is the source of all time, space, and beings. Can the source be confined by its emanations? God is the thinker and we are the thoughts. Can the thinker be comprehended by the thought? Can the eye see itself? Can the ear hear itself? Just as you cannot see your own eye, because your eye is the source of your seeing, so you cannot know God, because God is the source of your knowing. People think they can't see God because He is so far away. Quite the opposite: it is impossible to see God because He is too close. We yearn for our source, but the thought form cannot think of the thinker.

This recognition is very humbling. Yet it is possible for us to "know" God. It takes tremendous humility to know God, because we have to let go of our demand to have a well-formulated, comprehensible concept at our mind's disposal. We have to stop trying to understand God in terms of time, space, and being. And we have to stop trying to know God as an object of our mind.

Knowing and Being Known

So, from our human perspective, God cannot be known. Both the usual process and the terminology of knowing are completely inappropriate when applied to the Divine. Until a person is ready to concede this, he or she cannot understand what Torah and Kabbalah mean when they refer to God.

We need a paradigm shift: I cannot know God as an object of thought, but I can *experience* God as the *subject* of all thought. This is the key to the first of four alternative ways of knowing God that I'm going to present.

How can I come to know my knower? By letting my knower know me. In other words, I can't come to know God, but I can experience being known by God.

The Talmud says that one should always be conscious that "there is an eye that sees and an ear that hears." Of course, it does not mean in a corporeal sense. It means that the sense of being known by God is an encounter with God. Many spiritual seekers pursue the goal of knowing God. In truth, the ultimate religious experience is an experience of being known by God. In fact, to exist means to be known by God. The more you realize that and live accordingly, the more substantial is your existence.

You know God experientially when you experience being known by God. Let's say you were in a deserted town, not a soul in sight, and you had the opportunity to steal anything you wanted without getting caught. Would you do it? If you would not do it, then that means you know that there is a soul in sight. That soul is you, and the sight is God's. A healthy soul intuits that what it does matters and is known by God.

Anytime you do something (or don't do something) because you are aware that "someone" is watching, you are experiencing God's knowledge of you, which essentially is a direct way to know of God.

How would you live your life if you lived with a constant awareness that what you do is known and matters to God? According to Kabbalah, the more you realize that what you do matters to God, the more substance there is to what you do.

Our goal is not to know the unknowable God but to feel permeated by God's knowledge of us.

If this seems like a very difficult concept to grasp, that is because it's not a concept, it's an experience. And it can't be grasped; it must be lived. This approach takes us to the very edge and end of perception. The end of perception is the experience of being perceived. When I look for God, I don't turn my attention to the vastness of outer space. Rather, I turn my attention to the vastness of inner space. I turn my attention to the source of all attention, all thought, all knowledge, and all consciousness. I seek the source of my mind, the Mind of all minds, Soul of all souls, the Self of all selves.

The Bible, in the Book of Genesis, begins with the words "In the beginning God created heaven and earth. . . ." When you think about it, this is quite an assumption. The Bible does not start off with very brilliant proofs for the existence of God, nor with philosophical introductions about the nature of God. This is because the Torah espouses that God is self-evident. Not just obvious, but *self*-evident. The way I can know God is the same way I know myself—from deep inside. Just as I am self-evident to myself, so too God (who is the Self of all self) is self-evident to me as the source of myself.

The problem is that most people are looking for the wrong God. They are looking for an object—an idol. They want to see the God whom everyone has been talking about, the eternal, infinite being who floats in outer space.

I once read that the first cosmonaut who went into space was asked by the ground station, "What do you see?" He responded, "I don't see God." An eternal infinite being working from outer space is not self-evident. But God who is the Self of all selves is self-evident.

It is self-evident that consciousness doesn't start with me or end with me. I may have the choice to decide what I want to think about, but I have no choice concerning the fact that I think at all. Therefore, if I am not the source of consciousness, who is? If I am not the master of consciousness, who is? Whoever is, I give the name God.

THE FAME GAME

To know God I must experience being known by God. In fact, just to exist, I must be known. This is why people have an innate need to be acknowledged. Being acknowledged is the foundation of our existence. My daughter, swinging from a jungle gym, yells out to me, "Daddy, look!" It is not so much that she wants my praise, but on some level she senses that someone witnessing her feat makes it real. That is also why children run away from home: so that someone will look for them. If you ever ran away as a child, you would remember the terrible fear that maybe no one would notice your absence; maybe no one would come looking for you. The very fact of being "looked for" reinforces the developing identity of the young child.

Once I was walking in Jerusalem when I noticed a large crowd gathered around some kind of spectacle. I, too, tried to get a glimpse of what everyone was gawking at. To my surprise it was only two punk rockers sitting on the corner. One had green hair and safety pins pierced through his eyebrows and nostrils. The other had a rooster-top hairdo and tattoos all over his body. For Jerusalem they were really unusual. I wondered why people do this to themselves. But then I realized that they were simply yearning for attention. They needed to feel that their existence was acknowledged. And in truth we all do because the very foundation of our existence is God's acknowledgment. The problem is that human acknowledgement can never really give us the ultimate satisfaction we want.

Is it really important that I be known by you? You and I are both temporal. We could be here today and gone tomorrow. Besides, human acknowledgment can never be enough. Kirk Douglas relates a story of an early role he played on Broadway. The reviews were outstanding. One critic praised Kirk's performance and said that he was "nothing short of superb." But Kirk's reaction wasn't a happy one. That night, lying in bed, he couldn't sleep. "What do they mean '*nothing* short of'? If they think I'm superb, why don't they just come right out and say so!"

Human acknowledgement will never be enough because our very existence depends on *God's* acknowledgment.

The first question Larry King asked me in an interview on his show was "Is God watching us?" I thought I would crack a joke. Something like, "Larry, every day millions of people watch *Larry King Live*. How could God miss your show?" I chose not to risk the humor. So I simply said: "Yes, God is watching us all the time. It's the basis of our existence."

Before the show I was really excited. Millions of people around the globe were going to watch me on television. The thrill, however, lasted only a short while after the show. Although such opportunities are fun, they do not transform the quality of your existence. Whether millions watch you or not, you will still exist. What really matters is to know that God is watching you. If people turn off their TV during the Larry King show, Larry will continue to be. But if God stops watching Larry King, then there is no more *Larry King Live*.

Kabbalah teaches us that the more we believe that God is watching us and express that belief in our actions and interactions with each other, the more we will actually experience that truth. We will feel God's loving guidance and care in our daily life.

True fulfillment in life does not come from winning world recognition and achieving fame. There are plenty of famous people who are miserable. True fulfillment comes through knowing that God knows you and cares. When you realize that this is the true foundation of life, then your priorities in life are different. You are less concerned with what others think about you and more concerned with simply being good and doing the right things. You are motivated to do acts that are worthy of God's attention. You would say a kind word to the taxi driver today.

You would call up a friend just to see how he or she is doing. You would gladly make a donation to a good cause or a homeless person on the street. These acts are not newsworthy. They won't get you on the front page of the *New York Times*. And they will not be remembered forever by the public. Even the recipient of your kindness may forget you. But these acts make the headlines in heaven, and God will never forget you. These small deeds may not be newsworthy, but they are noteworthy. Because God, so to speak, will take note and inscribe you in the Book of Life. This is the secret to real happiness. Keep in mind that you are in God's mind. And remember you exist because God thinks and cares about you. In other words, you exist because God minds.

Therefore, the true path to knowing God is to experience being known by God. And if you want to experience being known by God, then act as if you *are* known by God. Do what God asks of you.

According to the Torah, spiritual search is not about trying to find an image of God, but rather about searching for God's image of you. When the first chapter of Genesis declares that God created man in His image, it is telling us what life is all about: not finding God's image, but being God's image, a reflection and expression of God.

A person who is truly a reflection and expression of God knows God. A person who philosophizes about God knows nothing, because God cannot be known as an object. God can only be known as the subject of all expressions—just as the thinker is expressed and reflected in his thought, or the musician is expressed and reflected in her song.

Our goal as human beings is not to behold a vision of God, who cannot be envisioned, but to *become* the vision of God, to actually be the way God envisions us.

THE PATH OF SERVICE

We know God as the subject not only through being known by God but also through being used by God.

I once met a very successful film writer in Hollywood. He told me that every day, before he starts to write, he begins with a little prayer: "Please, God, use me." He explained to me that he never feels that he is writing the script. He experiences God writing through him. "These films are God's, not mine," he said. I told him, "The good ones are God's, but the bad ones are yours."

A friend of mine who writes novels shared a similar experience. She said that the most beautiful passages in her book were somehow "dictated" to her. She heard the words in her mind and simply wrote them down, struggling to type as fast as the words were coming.

Often, when I give public lectures, I actually hear a voice within me telling me what to say. The problem, however, is that it sometimes tells me to go in a different direction than what I have prepared in my written notes. I have learned to trust this voice and surrender, even though I do not know where it will take me. The lecture always comes out better than I planned. I also enjoy it much more because I experience God as the speaker and myself as the speaking.

A word of caution: if you start to think that whenever you give yourself over to an impulse, it is God acting or speaking through you, you can get into major trouble. This is why the Torah gives us direction and guidelines on how we can be truly in the service of God. And when we follow these directives, we plug into the source of all being.

This is expressed in the profound meaning of the essential name of God—YHVH, the Tetragrammaton. This name (as we mentioned earlier) comes from the Hebrew word that means "to be." One of the main principles of the Torah is that all names associated with God suggest something about God's action (though not His essence). YHVH suggests that the essential act of God is being. Therefore, perhaps the best translation of this name would be "be-er." If you are speaking, then you are a speaker. If you are writing, then you are a writer. And if you are being, then you are a "be-er."

This name reveals to us the amazing truth about ourselves. We are "beings." We are actually verbs.

What does it mean: "to be"?

Let's say that Joe is intelligent but he is not *being* intelligent. That would mean that he is not expressing and manifesting his intelligence. So, too, the entire universe is a verb—a dynamic process of expression. Who, then, is the noun? Who is the subject? Who is being? YHVH—the one and only Source of All Being, the Be-er.

When I realized that this would be the best translation of the Tetragrammaton, I looked into a dictionary to see if there was ever such a word. And indeed I found in the *Oxford Universal Dictionary* this definition: "Be-er: One who is, the Self-existent, the great I Am."

Yes, God is the Be-er, the source and subject of all being. But we are beings. We are verbs.

God is the Speaker and we are the speaking. God is the Knower and we are not only the known but also the knowing.

All genuine artists have experienced God as the subject, whether or not they identified Him as such. The sense of being a channel for a creative force that flows through one is an experience of God as the subject. Bob Dylan was once asked, "How do you write music?" He answered, "I just sit down to write, and I know it's going to be all right."

I sometimes write songs. Once I was sitting at my piano and started to play a beautiful song I had never heard before. I actually felt possessed; my fingers were moving without my telling them where to go. My wife walked into the room and asked, "What is this song?" I replied, "I don't know. I'm just trying to keep out of the way."

In such creative acts, artists experience that the painting or the poem or the dance is coming through them, not from them. The true source is somehow "beyond." This is an intuitive experience of God as the subject. In such moments of illumination we know God.

This is the true meaning behind all the commandments. We

come to know God through serving to actualize His will and be in His image. The commandments are like cables that connect us with the source of all consciousness.

When the Jewish people received the Torah at Mount Sinai, the first revelation they heard was really the compelling reason why they would gladly want to perform God's will. The first commandment is to know that "I am the Lord, your God, who took you out of Egypt."

However, this is not necessarily the only way to translate the original Hebrew text. It could also be translated as "The 'I' is the Lord your God, who took you out of Egypt." In other words, the Jewish people had the experience of the Ultimate "I," the one and only subject, God. When we plug into the Ultimate "I" by fulfilling the commandments, we access the ultimate power of freedom and creativity. Freedom from slavery is achieved through serving God. Serving God is actually *self*-serving, because God is the source of all self.

THE WAY OF REFLECTION

A third way of knowing God is through His reflection in this universe. Your eyes cannot see themselves, but they can see a reflection of themselves in a mirror, and that will give you some idea of what they look like. I cannot define God in terms of time, space, and created beings, but I can experience God as reflected in them.

For example, in looking at a Rembrandt painting, we don't imagine that we are seeing Rembrandt himself, but we can infer something about Rembrandt's character attributes by looking at his work. There is a piece of the master in his masterpiece. Thus, a certain refinement, good humor, and gentleness of character are obvious in Rembrandt's paintings, which tell us something about the person who wielded the brush, although the essence of the artist remains hidden from us.

Similarly, we can certainly see God's reflection in His work. The Book of Job (19:26) says: "Through my flesh I will see

God," meaning that by reflecting on the astounding intricacy of one's own body, one can learn much about God's attributes.

For example, one great sign of God's love for us is our saliva. Saliva not only contains antibacterial properties, but it softens our food so that we can swallow it without effort or pain. The six salivary glands perfectly positioned in every mouth did not have to be there. Human beings could eat, digest, and derive nutrition from their food without the salivary glands. Saliva makes the difference between the act of eating being pleasurable or not. That God created human beings with salivary glands in the mouth is an act of love. Eating is pleasurable because God wanted to give us that pleasure.

If your husband gives you a strictly utilitarian present, such as a food processor, you might question whether he loves you or your function as a gourmet cook; but if he gives you a beautiful necklace, which serves only to make you happy, you can infer his love for you. From just the saliva in our mouth, we can taste God's love for us.

The delightful variety of colors, shapes, and smells in a garden similarly attest to the love of the One who created such beauty for our enjoyment. Although scientists say that flowers are designed by nature simply to attract pollinators, surely anyone who beholds a delicate red rose or smells the fragrance of jasmine feels that these are God's gifts to humanity. When I smell a gardenia, I experience God's freely given love for me.

It is important to emphasize that nothing in the creation can enable me to describe the Creator's essence. His attributes may be reflected in His creation; His essence remains totally hidden. Nonetheless, if I reflect upon the wonders of the universe and the wonder of my very existence, I can experientially know God.

THE WAY OF THE PROPHET

The fourth method of knowing God is through prophetic revelation. Through using methods such as meditation and music, the prophets of ancient Israel were able to induce altered states of consciousness in which they experienced a direct revelation from God. In other words, the Knower communicated to the known. Sometimes they received a message for the entire world.

When such messages had eternal significance, they were recorded and later incorporated into the Hebrew Bible. Only fifteen prophets' revelations are included, with another dozen or so prophets mentioned by name in the various biblical books. The Talmud, however, tells us that there were as many prophets in ancient Israel as Israelites who came out of Egypt during the Exodus—approximately three million.

The Talmud also tells us that after the Temple was destroyed, the period of prophecy ended. Today we are able to experience divine inspiration, but not actual prophecy.

Divine inspiration is only a general message of guidance, in contrast to prophecy, which was a specific message of clear direction.

Prophetic revelation is the exact opposite of what we do when we seek an experience of God—which characterizes so much of the spiritual quest in our time. When we seek the vision of God, God is the object. In revelation, God is the subject; which means that God can tell a prophet something the prophet does not want to hear.

The prime example of this is the Book of Jonah. God told Jonah to go to Nineveh, and Jonah headed as fast as he could in the opposite direction, because he had major objections to preaching to the sinners of Nineveh. (That's why he ended up in the belly of that big fish.)

In contrast to a prophet, today's seekers of God perceive themselves as the subject, and their search will never take them beyond their own will or preferences.

Revelation is given knowledge. It is knowledge that guides us in our world according to God's perspective. Revelation begins where human experience ends. Experience can take me only to the outer limits of my own perspective. Revelation is information bestowed from a higher perspective.

The Torah claims that God revealed Himself to the entire

Israelite people at Mount Sinai. The commandments, or guiding instructions of the Torah, can never make complete sense from a human perspective, because the very definition of revelation is knowledge bestowed from a divine perspective.

To give a simple metaphor, revelation is like the traffic station on the radio. You are driving down route 83, and you wonder which is the quickest way to your destination. Is there a traffic jam ahead? Should you get off at the next exit and take an alternative route? Or take your chances with the traffic lights on the main thoroughfare? There is really no way for you to know; you cannot possibly see the next two miles of roadway. But the traffic helicopter hovering overhead sees everything. From its perspective, all the highways and traffic patterns are perfectly visible. So you tune in to the traffic station, and you hear the clear message: "Traffic jam on route 83 between Kilmer and Havington. If you're traveling north, exit at route 144." Even the most deluxe, state-of-the-art automobile can never know what the helicopter knows, unless the helicopter communicates to it. That is revelation.

Although revelation is information given to human beings from a higher perspective, the content of the revelation is still expressed in human terminology. Thus, when the Israelites experienced God directly at the splitting of the Red Sea, they saw Him as a warrior. At the revelation at Sinai, they experienced God as a wise sage. The prophet Ezekiel had a vision of God and saw the celestial chariot and throne. What is all this about? Had these people made the mistake of seeing God as an object?

Not at all. Prophetic revelation comes in the form of transcendental messages, which the human mind translates into images. Have you ever listened to a symphony while lying on the couch with your eyes closed? Sometimes, as you listen to the music, your mind's eye sees visual images. A certain airy section of flute or violin may conjure up in your mind the image of a butterfly. Turbulent sounds may invoke the image of a storm. Although your mind is translating the sounds into pictures, you know that neither the butterfly nor the storm is an actual picture of the sounds you are hearing. So, too, in revelation, the prophetic experience is translated into a picture, but the picture is no more a picture of God than the butterfly is a picture of those musical sounds.

In Summary

In summary, we must realize that when we search for God, we are looking for the source of time, space, and all creation. And we are looking for the source of all knowing. Therefore, our normative descriptive language and methods for knowing anything are not applicable to knowing the One who is the Source of Everything.

To know God we have to adopt completely new ways of knowing. We can know God by experiencing being known by God. We can know God through serving God and experiencing God as the ultimate subject—the source of all being. We can know God through reflecting on the wonders of this universe and getting a glimpse of the Master in His masterpiece. And we can know God through the prophetic experience whereby God communicates to us directly—the Knower communicates to the known.

9

To Serve,
Grow, Love,
and Know

LET US NOW PULL IT all together, do a quick overview, and take a look at the big picture.

Can the perfect God become perfect? Yes and no.

God, the Absolute Perfect One, when described from our limited human perspective, has the possibility to manifest two types of perfection: *being* perfect, which is static and never-changing, and *becoming* perfect, which is dynamic and ever-changing.

When, so to speak, God freely chose to actualize the possibility of becoming perfect, then there had to be an imperfection as the foundation for a dynamic process of growth and becoming toward more and more perfection. Therefore, God created the imperfect human being in this imperfect world and inspirited him/her with a spark of Himself—the soul. In other words, God lives His secret life on earth through you and me because we are sparks of His very Self.

Can God fail, suffer, feel sadness, make mistakes, struggle with evil, and strive to become more perfect, choose the good, overcome the challenges, grow, and celebrate victory? Yes. Through you and me.

God participates in the challenges of life on earth through you and me. God shares our pains and struggles, ups and downs, the good times and the bad, because we are sparks of God. We are not God, but we are an aspect of God. And we must always remember that although God is manifest within us, He is also beyond us. However, the more we invite God into our life through prayer and through performing His commandments, the more we experience God living His secret life through us.

The commandments are directives from God, but more than that, they are actually an assignment by God. They are a statement of the mission to be performed on God's behalf by us human beings on earth. When you accept the mission of the commandments, you become God's agent on earth, just as angels are God's agents but in heaven.

We qualify for this mission because we are able to make so many mistakes and struggle with evil. We are inundated with problems and challenges from within and without. We are perfect for this job because we are so imperfect!

Our mission is to reveal a dynamic perfection of becoming, to overcome our failings, choose goodness, and grow for God's sake.

When we accept our divine mission, we not only do a service to God but we do a service to ourselves. When we fulfill God's commandments, we solve our existential crisis of insecurity and experience the significance of our true self. Otherwise we feel like nothing—useless and disposable.

The distinction between God and us human beings is that God's existence is absolute and necessary, but human existence is mere possibility. In a manner of speaking, we would say that

God has to be, but God does not have to create you and me. We do not have to be. We are manifestations of God's free will. And God at any moment could choose to no longer express dynamic perfection.

This idea is the foundation of our great human dilemma, of our existential crisis, our insistence on our significance, and yet our struggle with our disposability. We are paradoxically unnecessary manifestations of the necessary. That's why there is something about us that feels disposable, and yet there is something to that feeling that we are absolute and necessary. And here lies the root of our dilemma.

Freedom gives us pleasure, and freedom gives us pain. It expresses who we are—manifestations of God's free will. But it also reminds us of who we are—mere possibility.

Commandments solve our conflict between the desire for freedom and the desire to feel that who we are and what we do is necessary. When we freely choose to do what we must do and dedicate ourselves to serving the One who must be, then we reveal and experience the truth about ourselves, which we intuited all along—we are sparks of the absolute God. We then feel filled with a profound sense of security and peace.

What is our real mission in life? How free are we to determine the events and achievements of our lives toward becoming more perfect? And to what extent does God really run the world?

Free choice is the very basis of a life guided by the commandments. The essence of commandments is that you can choose to obey them or disobey them and enjoy the rewards of your choice or suffer the consequences. Without free choice there could be no commandments, no liability for our actions, no struggle, no mission, and no meaning to life. If everything were determined, if everything had been plotted out by God already, then we would simply be puppets, and the consequences we enjoy or suffer from our actions would be arbitrary.

However, there are many traditional Jewish sources that

point to a shocking amount of determinism in the world, which would seem to suggest that we are not free at all.

Therefore, we must ask: Is the story of life a monologue, in which God is like an author talking in many different voices to Himself through his characters, whose lives are totally determined? Or is the story of life a dialogue, in which we interact with God and contribute to the story through our free choices?

The answer is yes and yes.

Free choice and determinism both exist simultaneously—the story of life is beyond either/or.

This is the mystery of history. Both sides of the paradox are true. Life is a monologue, predetermined and written by God. But mysteriously it is also a dialogue written by God and us through the free choices we make. It's beyond the either/or.

Our ultimate choice, however, is choice itself and the awareness it accomplishes. Every scene of life is all about the choices we make, the awareness we achieve, the meaning we give to every situation, the lessons we learn, the attitudes we adopt, and the qualities of holiness, kindness, fairness, honesty, compassion, integrity, and forgiveness that we embody. In other words, our real task is to change our inner world and become a *living* reflection of God's image. Our goal as human beings is to become, so to speak, a mirror for God. The commandments enable us to actualize the divine image that we were created to be and thereby reflect the attributes of God. When we achieve that, it is as if we connect the circuit of God's self-reflection and knowledge of His oneness. This is our role in the divine drama, whose theme is the process of God's self-refection and knowledge. In this process, oneness becomes conscious.

Although God is one, does God know that She/He is one? Does God experience His/Her oneness? Does God have the choice to become one? Of course, the answer is: yes and no. We exist because the answer is also yes, and we have been given the mission to acknowledge God's oneness and reveal it. Our mission is to realize that we are in essence one with each other and one with God.

This is what it really means to serve God—to be God's agent and work on His behalf to facilitate this divine process, whereby the One becomes conscious through free choice. That is why the significance of our choices is measured not by how we affect what is going on around us, but by what happens within us. The focus of our choices is about how to change ourselves, become living reflections of God, and achieve a higher awareness of God's oneness.

What is the true meaning of God's oneness? The oneness of God is not like the oneness in our dictionary. It's not like the number one. The oneness of God does not mean only one as opposed to two or three. The oneness of God is actually non-duality. It is not the opposite of many. It is a oneness that includes both one and many, where the One is in the many and many are in the One.

The closest experience we have that delivers to us a taste of God's oneness is love. In love, two can be one and yet two.

In truth, God is always one, and we are always one with God and with each other. The problem is that this truth is hidden by the worlds of perception. We live in the lowest world of perception. Therefore, all that we see is fragmentation and multiplicity. This world encourages attitudes of selfishness, deceit, hate, competition, and war.

Our challenge and our work are to ascend the ladder of consciousness and achieve an *awareness* of God's oneness and experience love.

Why did God hide His oneness? For oneness to become conscious, it must first be hidden. Therefore, the hiding of the oneness is for the very purpose of becoming revealed. God has hidden Himself, His oneness, from us so that we can find it, realize it, and experience love. However, since you and I are sparks of God, then it is as if God is hiding Himself from an aspect of Himself. Therefore, our journey in search of the One is on behalf of the One and for the sake of the One. Our job is to serve God in His process of self-reflection and knowledge of His oneness and experience the ecstasy of love.

When we fulfill the commandments we are, so to speak, uniting the manifestation of the Divine within us with the manifestation of the Divine beyond us. We are like a switch that can either break the circuit of God's self-reflection that reveals God's mysterious oneness (that is both beyond and within the many) or connect the circuit. Then the light of love shines.

This is the journey of our lives. This is the journey God has sent us on. This is our divine mission—to reveal the hidden One and experience love.

In the time of redemption, when our consciousness will evolve to the highest perspective, the highest world, we will actually perceive the oneness of God as it truly is. "God will be one and His name will be one." In that time we will burst into laughter, realizing that all the hiddenness and darkness actually empowered us to see the light and reveal God's oneness. We will then know that only love is real.

But of course, love is not a destiny. You can always love more and more. Therefore, love is an endless journey.

This love story never ends.

In Summary

We are vehicles for God's expression of and participation in a process of becoming perfect. We imperfect human beings are in this imperfect world to do a divine mission. The Torah and the commandments define that mission. Without that divine mission, we are insecure and feel like nothing. We find inner peace and security when we choose to do what we must do for the One who must be, because in this way we express and experience our true self—the soul, a spark of the Absolute. The commandments enable us to become the living reflection of God, so to speak, a mirror for God. Our ultimate goal and only true accomplishment is to serve God in His process of self-reflection and knowledge of His oneness. Then we will achieve the joyous experience of love.

We are secret agents in the secret life of God. God lives His secret life on earth through you and me—if we let Him in.

Our mission is to serve, grow, love, and know.

This is our ultimate purpose, power, passion, and pleasure.

Invitation to the Reader

DEAR READER,

Please feel free to write me. It would be an honor and a pleasure to receive your comments and questions.

All the best,

David Aaron
    c/o Isralight
    25 Misgav Ladach
    Old City, Jerusalem
    97500
    Israel

E-mail: david.aaron@isralight.org

For more information about Isralight seminars, retreats, and articles by Rabbi David Aaron, see www.isralight.org.

Index

About the Author

RABBI DAVID AARON, the son of a Holocaust survivor, has struggled since early youth to understand the world's potential for hatred and paradoxical yearning for meaning, love, and creativity. His own spiritual journey led him to Israel, where he studied Torah and Jewish mysticism under the tutelage of the great masters. He received his rabbinical ordination in 1979 from the Israel Torah Research Institute (ITRI). A popular lecturer in North America and a frequent guest on radio and TV, David Aaron is the founder and dean of Isralight (www.isralight.org), an international organization with centers and programs throughout North America and in Israel. Rabbi Aaron lives in Jerusalem with his wife, Chana, and their seven children.

David Aaron's other books include *Endless Light: the Ancient Path of the Kabbalah to Love, Spiritual Growth, and Personal Power* (1997, 1998) and *Seeing God: Ten Life-Changing Lessons of the Kabbalah* (2001, 2002).